Steph
Winw

How to Talk with God

the dynamics of prayer

Harold Shaw Publishers
Wheaton, Illinois

6th printing January 1977

ISBN 0-87788-360-2
Library of Congress catalog card number 72-93098
Printed in the United States of America
First North American Edition

contents

INTRODUCTION

"Prayer is the Christian's vital breath, the Christian's native air." This truth is widely acknowledged by those "who profess and call themselves Christians," as a result of the efforts of our preachers and teachers, who often tell us to pray. But to teach the vital importance of prayer, and to exhort and urge men to pray, is insufficient. There is too much general exhortation and far too little practical instruction. More attention should be given to *how to talk with God.* Again and again the average busy person asks, "How can I converse with God, and live in unbroken fellowship with Him in this twentieth century?" Although this book contains a good deal of teaching and a little exhortation, it is not a theoretical treatise about prayer. It is concerned throughout with the practice of prayer. The keyword is *how*.

Following the two general introductory chapters "Why Pray?" and "How to Learn," the rest of the book can be divided into four main parts. Chapters

3 and 4 are entirely concerned with those special periods of personal prayer, the daily morning and evening Quiet Times, which are the basis of the devotional life. The chief kinds of prayer—Adoration, Thanksgiving, Repentance, Petition, Intercession—are then described in Chapters 7 to 10, with special reference to those Quiet Times. The third main division, Chapters 11 to 13 could be given the title "Total Prayer"—how to pray with the whole personality and with the whole Church. In the last part of the book, Chapters 14 and 15, we consider how to express our devotion to God in ways other than prayer—our conduct, work, and life in the world.

My indebtedness to other writers is acknowledged in the footnotes. The Scripture quotations are from the Revised Standard Version of the Bible, copyrighted 1946 and 1952 by the Division of Christian Education, National Council of Churches, U.S.A., and used by permission.

Stephen F. Winward

WHY PRAY?

1

Why learn to talk with God? Why study a book about it, or give up some time each day to the practice of prayer? It is easy to see why a man should want to teach himself carpentry. He may want to become a carpenter and to earn his living that way. He may take it up as a hobby, an enjoyable recreation. Or there may be a combination of motives—he will enjoy the work, augment his income, make furniture for the home and gifts for his friends. But why bother to learn how to pray? Is it really necessary? Apparently not, for many people today seem to get along quite well in this world without it. Is it then a kind of hobby, like gardening or bird-watching, an optional extra to the main business of living, for which some people have an inclination or aptitude?

We shall often be tempted to believe that prayer is no use, or that it is not enjoyable. Why then should we pray? We must be clear about this from the start. If we are to accept the discipline of prayer, we must have adequate incentives. We are likely to keep at it only if we believe the effort is really worthwhile. In this chapter we shall discover four main reasons for prayer.

Prayer is fellowship with God

Man has been created for God, and only in fellowship with God can he find fulness of life. It is hard for us to define what life is; but we do know that it exists only in *relationship.* A stone is dead, a horse is alive—a stone cannot enter into relationship with its environment, a horse can. A man can enter into relationship not only with nature, but also with other people in the life of his community. If all his personal relationships could be broken, he would be negated as a personal being. The richness of our personal life depends upon the quality and depth of our personal relationships. The highest relationship possible to man is fellowship with God, apart from which his relationship with nature and with people can never be right and harmonious, satisfying and complete. This relationship is life—a new or higher quality of life; it is eternal life.

In human life we enter into relationship with other people through meeting and conversation. Nowadays, much communication takes place at a distance either through the written word, or through the word spoken over the telephone, radio, or television. But usually we get to know people and enter into fellowship with them through direct encounter and conversation. This is also true of the highest relationship possible to man. It is by meeting and talking with God—that is, by prayer—that we enter into relationship with God, and come to know Him more and more deeply.

This does not mean that we can have no knowledge of God at all apart from prayer. Even the prayerless man has to be related in some way to "Him in whom we live, and move, and have our being." Our relationship to nature and especially to people is always, if indirectly, a reflection of our attitude toward God, even if it is an attitude of indifference or rejection. But a direct personal relationship with God depends upon meeting and conversation. A man who never prays may know a lot about God. Only the man who prays can *know God.* This is the strongest incentive to prayer, and its greatest reward.

The analogy of human friendship is helpful here. Why do we talk with our friends? Not because they are useful to us or confer benefits upon us—although these are frequently among the by-products of friendship. The true reward of friendship is the friend himself. We appreciate his personality, enjoy his company and conversation, find enrichment and fulfillment in the fellowship of giving and receiving. Read the following words of the Psalmist, and it is clear that what he gets out of communion with God is, quite simply, *God.*

Whom have I in heaven but thee? And there is nothing on earth that I desire besides thee. My flesh and my heart may fail, but God is the strength of my heart and my portion for ever (Psalm 73:25, 26).

And so we pray in order to enter into, sustain, and deepen our fellowship with God, whom to know is life eternal.

Prayer is giving to God

Now this dialog, this conversation with God which is prayer, has two aspects; it is a fellowship of giving and receiving. Just as in a mature human relationship there is give and take, so in the activity of prayer we give to and receive from God. Because of who God is, we receive, or should receive, far more from Him than we can ever give to Him. However, there can be no mature relationship with God apart from both giving and receiving. The giving aspect of prayer is best expressed in the word "offering."

In the Bible, worship is essentially something offered to God accompanied by praise and thanksgiving, penitence and petition. We pray in order to give something to God our Creator and Redeemer. "Ascribe to the Lord glory and strength! Ascribe to the Lord the glory due His name; bring an offering and come into His courts" (Psalm 96:7, 8). We are to offer *praise*, to adore Him, to acknowledge His worth, to appreciate and enjoy what He is in Himself. We are to offer the sacrifice of *thanksgiving*, acknowledging with gratitude all the gifts of God in creation, providence, and redemption. We are to offer *repentance*, the sacrifice of a broken and contrite heart, the humble confession of our imperfection, failure, and sinfulness. We are to offer *ourselves,* to present our bodies as a living sacrifice, holy and acceptable to God. Man was made for God, and by giving ourselves to Him in adoration and thanksgiving, in repentance and obedience, we fulfill the purpose and the chief end of our being.

Prayer is receiving from God

When King David was offering gifts to God for the building of the Temple, he said, "All things come from thee, and of thy own have we given thee" (I Chronicles 29:14). We can only give to God what we have already received from Him. Prayer cannot be an offering, unless it is first a receiving. We come to God like a woman to the well, with an empty vessel to be filled from the sparkling source of all wisdom, power, and love. God wills to give us Himself, and on the human side prayer is opening the door to the Lord who stands and knocks, so that He may come in and have fellowship with us. It is important for us to understand that in prayer we are to receive the Lord Himself, not just His gifts.

If we come to God in prayer only when *we want something,* we are like a boy who goes to his father only when he wants spending money. Instead, we are to go to God to receive Him anew into our lives. This receiving happens in many ways—by waiting on Him in silence, by reading or hearing

His word, through meditation, in the sacraments, and above all in those prayers in which we ask that we may receive. If our first concern is to receive God Himself, then we shall rightly and gladly receive His gifts as well.

Our asking for these may take the form of "make me" or of "give me." First we ask that God's grace may create or strengthen within us those graces and virtues, those qualities of character and those abilities which will enable us to live the life of God. But it is God's will that *all* our needs—not only our character needs—should be supplied, material as well as spiritual. By making us what we should be and giving us what we need, God, through our prayer, supplies us with every resource for life. This adequacy, this sufficiency, this supply of needed power and resource for living, is one of the rewards of faithful prayer. Even during our prayers of giving we are receiving, for as we offer ourselves to God, we open our inmost selves to Him, and give Him the opportunity for which He is always waiting, to give Himself and His gifts to us. Thus prayer is the fellowship of giving and receiving.

Prayer is co-operation with God

St. Augustine said something which gives concise expression to one of the fundamental reasons for prayer. "Without God we cannot: without us God will not." God wills to work in partnership with man, and He has so ordered the world that this co-operation is essential. God works among men, not apart from men, but through men. There are many things we cannot do without God; there are many things God will not do without us. The farmer cannot create a harvest, however hard he works; but God does not give him a harvest unless he works. Now this co-operation with God is to take place not only through our work, but also through our prayer. It is no exaggeration to say that prayer is the most important way in which we can co-operate with God. It is the supreme way of knowing God's will, and of bringing our wills into harmony with His will. For the object of prayer is not to persuade God to do what I want, but to enable me to know, desire, and do what He wants. Like Christ in Gethsemane, we are to pray that God's will may be done, done not only by me—but by all men. Prayer is co-operation with God's purpose in and through the lives of others; it is intercession for the whole creation. It is man working together with God for the achievement of His age-long purpose: "*Thy* kingdom come, thy will be done, on earth, as it is in heaven."

Remember that:

1. We pray in order that we may live in fellowship with God.

2. We pray in order that we may give to God His due—our offerings of praise, thanksgiving, repentance, and an obedient life.

3. We pray in order that we may receive God and

His gifts into our lives.

4. We pray in order that we may co-operate with God in achieving His purpose for all mankind.

HOW TO LEARN
TO PRAY

2

Do we really need to *learn* how to pray? After all, some may say prayer is an inborn tendency, a natural activity of man. As such it is spontaneous and unlearned. We do not have to learn how to breathe; we begin to do it almost as soon as we are born. It is an innate activity, prior to all thought, learning, and experience. And it is obvious that the men of God in past ages did not study prayer *as a subject,* in order to learn how to do it. We cannot imagine Abraham sitting in his tent or Moses tending the sheep in the desert, being concerned with the method and technique of prayer! They just prayed—and they obviously knew how to pray. William James has said "Many reasons have been given why we should not pray, whilst others are given why we should. But in all this very little is said of the reason why we do pray. The reason why we pray is simply that we cannot help praying." Why do we need to *learn* how to do something which is so spontaneous, inevitable, and natural to man?

Natural activity and learning

It is, of course, a mistake to assume that because an activity is natural (a question-begging word), it does not have to be learned, or cannot be improved by further learning. It is natural for a human being to walk, but we are not born with the ability to do so. We learn to walk, usually with the help and encouragement of others, and only after much practice and many falls. The analogy of speech is even more illuminating, since prayer itself is conversation with God. Speech is natural to man, and yet we all have to learn how to talk meaningfully. And, unlike walking, in which most normal people reach about the same level of proficiency, people differ enormously in the extent to which they master language and conversation—from the person who can hardly put two words together, to the gifted conversationalist or orator.

Prayer is natural to unfallen man, and to fallen man in certain circumstances; yet like speech between men, it must be learned. Certainly Abraham and Moses did not learn how to pray from a book or in a classroom—there are other ways of learning—but they had to learn. If we refuse to take the trouble to learn how to pray, then even if we go on praying, our prayers will be immature and childish (which is not the same as childlike). It is by no means rare for people of high intelligence and wide experience to continue to pray in adult life just as they were taught in childhood at their mother's knee. They would be unable to say of their prayers

HOW TO LEARN TO PRAY   17

"When I was a child, I spoke like a child, I thought like a child, I reasoned like a child; when I became a man I gave up childish ways" (I Corinthians 13:11). To become full-grown in this sphere, it is necessary to give thought and time to the study and practice of prayer. How can we learn to pray?

Learning by doing

In most realms of life, we learn by doing; this is the most basic and important way of learning. We cannot learn to swim by studying a text-book on swimming. The learner must get into the water and make the attempt. This is not to say that theory or technique is worthless. It is often helpful and sometimes essential; but it is rarely sufficient in itself. The medical student must study his textbooks, but that alone will never make him a proficient doctor. Some skills are acquired almost entirely by practice—typing, playing tennis, driving a car.

This is undoubtedly the most important way of learning how to pray: in the school of life, by practice. It is by praying consistently and often that we best learn how to pray. The skill of the professional football player seems to the unthinking spectator to be "natural", but in fact it "comes naturally" only as a result of long and arduous practice.

Paderewski, the famous Polish pianist, once said "If I stop practicing the piano for a day, I notice the difference; if I stop for two days, my family notices the difference; if I stop for three days my friends notice the difference; and if I stop for a week the public notices the difference." In prayer, as in any kind of learning by doing, we shall make many mistakes, get "fed up," and fail again and again. But these mistakes and failures, as in learning to ride a bicycle or to speak French, can be a valuable part of the learning process. Resolve to put into daily practice all that you know about prayer, and all that you read in this book which applies to your own life and situation. Just as some of the problems of life are solved not only by thinking them out, but by living them out, so the art of prayer is learned, and its difficulties overcome, by praying.

Learning by doing it with others

Some things we learn by doing them alone—but a man could hardly become good at football by playing alone. He must practice, but with his team. We did not learn to speak our own language in isolation. As babies and infants we grew up in a family in which English was spoken by our parents. We listened to and imitated their words, and learned how to talk by doing it with them. We learn how to talk to God in the same way. It may be that we first learned to pray with our parents besides our beds or in family prayers, and then we learned to pray with the larger family of God in our church. In prayer groups and in worship together, in psalms and hymns, through liturgical or free prayer, we learn to pray not only by using the prepared language of others, but by doing it *with* others. Private and public, personal and corporate prayer, belong together. From the accumulated experience of the Christian community, the individual may derive stimulus, enrichment, and help.

Learning from scripture and from Christ

"The Lord used to speak to Moses face to face, as a man speaks to his friend" (Exodus 33:11). Spoken of Moses, these words are also true of many of the great men and women of the Bible. They walked with God as intimate friends, listening to His voice and talking to Him in prayer. We can learn from their experience, and in some cases from their recorded prayers. This is especially true of our Lord Jesus Christ, whose fellowship with the Father was unclouded, perfect, unique. On one occasion, sensing the depth and quality of His prayer life, the disciples came to Him with the request "Lord, teach us to pray" (Luke 11:1). Not only in the Lord's Prayer, the pattern which He gave to them in response, but in other sayings and parables, the teaching of Christ on prayer has been given to us. But He not only taught us how to pray—He prayed Himself.

Learning from books

Saved, taught, and inspired by Christ, many devout men and women in other ages, following in His steps, have trodden that same pathway of prayer. The prayer knowledge and experience of some of them has come down to us in writing. This precious legacy of autobiography and biography, of prayers and devotional classics, of letters and books about prayer, can inform and enrich our devotional thought and practice today. A wise learner does not start off from nothing, ignoring all that has already been discovered on his subject. He makes good use of the books written by others, attempting to assimilate all possible knowledge on the subject, as the basis of original research and experiment. So with prayer. And even by making use, on occasion, of the prayer-books of others, we can enlarge and enrich our own prayer life.

Learning from the Holy Spirit

One of the reasons why God gives to us the Holy Spirit to dwell within our hearts is that He may teach us how to pray. Recognizing that we do not know how to pray as we ought, the Lord comes to our aid, and teaches us from within. "Likewise the Spirit helps us in our weakness; for we do not know how to pray as we ought, but the Spirit himself intercedes for us with sighs too deep for words" (Romans 8:26). Christ taught His disciples how to pray; the Holy Spirit, continuing His work in the world, teaches us how to pray. Of course, the Spirit does not work in a vacuum; He teaches us through Scripture, and through the worship and devotional heritage of the Church. But He also operates from within the heart of the believer, inspiring thoughts of praise and holy desires, giving to us both the impulse and the content of prayer. That is why free or spontaneous prayer is so important. We must not "quench the Spirit," but leave room for His inspired spontaneity, praying as taught by God, who is working deep within us, both to will and to work His good pleasure.

Remember that:

There are five main ways in which you can learn to talk with God:

1. You learn to pray by praying, by acting upon what you already know, by daily practice.

2. You learn to pray by praying with others in the worshipping community.

3. You learn to pray from God's textbook, the Bible, especially from the teaching and example of Jesus Christ.

4. You learn to pray by reading and studying the devotional writings of others, and by making a judicious use of prayer-books.

5. You learn to pray by being alert and responsive to the inspiration of the Holy Spirit in your heart.

THE WHEN
AND WHERE
OF PRAYER

3

In Chapter 1, prayer was described as fellowship with God, in which we give ourselves to Him, receive Him and His gifts into our lives, and co-operate with Him so that His purposes in our lives and in the world may be fulfilled. But isn't it possible to do all this without having fixed or definite times of prayer? The whole of life should be a walk with God, and all times and all places should be sacred to Him. Might it not be better to have no fixed or special times of prayer, but to pray as often as possible, on impulse, or when the need arises, or the circumstances are especially fitting?

It is true that we should never *confine* our prayers to special times. We are told to "Pray without ceasing." Brother Lawrence, whose joyful desire was to be always with God, could even say, "The time of business does not with me differ from the time of prayer; and in the noise and clatter of my kitchen, while several persons are at the same time calling for different things, I possess God in as great tranquillity as if I were upon my knees at the blessed sacrament." By "the practice of the presence of God," all life can become communion with God, and by doing all things for Him, our daily work can be part of worship. The question is, how is it possible to reach, or at least move towards such an objective? How can the ideal be made a reality in our lives?

The part for the whole

Here we find an important principle: by the consecration of one special part, it is possible for us to consecrate the whole. If all the days of the week are to be holy, then one day of the week, the Lord's Day, must be set aside, must be holy to the Lord in a special way. But suppose I do not observe Sunday on the ground that all days are equally sacred. Then what happens? Do those who fail to observe the Lord's Day live dedicated lives on Wednesdays and Saturdays? So also, if the whole of a day is to be holy, then it is necessary to set aside, to dedicate, some part of it in a special way to God. Brother Lawrence was able to say "The time of business does not with me differ from the time of prayer" *because he observed the time of prayer.* It was "when the appointed times of prayer were past" that "he found no difference, because he still continued with God." He did not reach the true objective of devotion by ignoring the appointed times of prayer, but by observing them.

Jesus' example

As we discovered in Chapter 2, one of the ways in which we learn how to pray is by following the example of our Lord Jesus Christ. The whole of His life was one great act of prayer—intimate fellowship, perfect offering, complete co-operation with His Father. He alone lived the perfect life of total praise. But even He did not realize this objective without forming definite habits, the observance of special times of prayer. The gospels are not complete biographies; we have only a selection of the deeds of Jesus. Even so, there are suggestive hints and indications. Scholars have suggested that in Mark 1:21-39 the writer is describing a *typical* day in the life of Jesus. It includes the statement in verse 35, "And in the morning, a great while before day, he rose and went out to a lonely place, and there he prayed." And after miraculously feeding five thousand people, Jesus withdrew for prayer in the evening. "And after he had dismissed the crowds, he went up into the hills by himself to pray. When evening came, he was there alone" (Matthew 14:23). We know why Jesus withdrew into the Garden of Gethsemane "on the night when He was betrayed." It was to pray. But was that the only time? "Now Judas, who betrayed him, also knew the place; for Jesus *often* met there with his disciples" (John 18:2). And He who prayed in the mornings and the evenings, had also established the weekly habit of public prayer. "He went to the synagogue as his *custom* was, on the

Sabbath day" (Luke 4:16). If definite times of prayer were necessary even for the Son of God, is it likely that any of us will succeed in living the Christian life without them?

Having time means making time

The pace of life in this twentieth century makes it all the more necessary that we should follow the Lord's example of habitual prayer. For most of us, life is full, busy, hectic. There are not enough hours in the day, not enough days in the week, to pack in all that we have to do—or feel compelled to do. Life can easily degenerate into a relentless round of duties and pleasures, a frantic rushing here and there. If we expect prayer to fit into the appropriate time—well, it just won't fit. There is no appropriate time. It is simply crowded out. We become like Martha of Bethany, preoccupied with preparing an elaborate meal, when one course would have been enough. "Distracted with much serving" and "anxious and troubled about many things," she had no time to sit at the feet of Jesus and listen to his words (Luke 10:38-42). If we are to have time, we must make time. We must deliberately set it aside. Are some other things crowded out? Does it matter? It would be better to crowd out anything but God, since we have been created for Him.

When to pray

It is helpful to have a schedule of prayer: to set

aside certain definite times each day for meeting and talking with the Lord. Daniel "got down upon his knees three times a day and prayed and gave thanks before his God" (Daniel 6:10). The apostles also observed the set hours of prayer (see Acts 3:1, and 10:9). Such a rule should be a help and a guide, not a master or tyrant. It should not be rigid and legalistic. There are times when it is reasonable to set aside such a plan—perhaps because of sickness or urgent duties or needs. It may be wrong to insist on a time of prayer if it interferes with our obligations to others—on the other hand, it will certainly be wrong if it does *not* interfere with our own laziness and lack of self-discipline. We should regard these fixed times as appointments with the Lord, to be kept.

Now we should not generalize about such a schedule of prayer, because the character and temperament, the needs and circumstances of each individual are unique. Each one of us must make his own plan. But there is one important principle we should all bear in mind in making it. It is self-evident and fitting that we should begin and end each day with the Lord. We may be able to have other Quiet Times during the day, but we should all aim at starting and finishing each day in communion with God. Each separate day is then set in the framework of prayer, with a view to consecrating all that lies between. "From the rising of the sun to its setting, the name of the Lord is to be praised" (Psalm 113:3).

Morning prayer

So much of what we read, hear, and learn about prayer is negated by our failure to get up at the right time in the morning. For it is only by rising in time that there can be adequate time for prayer at the beginning of the day. This is especially true of all who have to start work at a definite hour. If I don't get up in time, I have no time for prayer; and if I haven't time for prayer, I shall not pray—it's as simple as that. A good alarm clock is a useful piece of equipment for the devotional life!

How much time should be given to morning prayer? Some find that they need an hour. Others are satisfied with half an hour, or twenty minutes. Those who find this an exceptionally hard discipline would be wise to aim at a minimum of ten minutes to begin with, and perhaps to increase it gradually. Whatever the length of time, it should never be hurried; we should not destroy the sense of leisure by trying to pack too much into it. Where should the morning Quiet Time fit into the pattern of the day? The ideal is to get up, wash, and dress first. This helps to ensure (especially if the water is cold!) that we are fully awake.

This ideal of morning prayer alone after dressing, before breakfast, may be difficult for those who share a room. It may be impossible for the mother with a baby to tend, or for the housewife who has to prepare a very early breakfast for her husband or children. Wives and mothers may find that the best time for prayer is immediately after the men have left for work or the children for school. Some have time to read and pray while commuting to work by bus or train. The best time for you—as close as possible to the beginning of the day—for at least ten minutes, and if you can for twenty or thirty minutes—these suggestions can be of help in planning your time with God.

Evening prayer

It is not so difficult to set aside time at the other end of the day for prayer. Work is done, and there is a sense of leisure, of lessening pressure. There is much more time available, for scripture reading, meditation, and prayer. And there is very great value in thinking of God and speaking to Him last thing at night. Our last thoughts sink down deeply into our minds and may continue to work within us while we sleep. "For he gives to his beloved in sleep" (Psalm 127:2).

On the other hand, there are others who habitually feel exhausted last thing at night. They find it difficult to keep awake and hard to concentrate. For these there may be an opportunity earlier, perhaps just after dinner, while the mind is still fresh and alert, for quiet reading and prayer.

The place of prayer

There is something to learn both from the teaching and the example of Christ about the place of prayer. Jesus did not think that all places were equally suitable—the street corner, for example!

"But when you pray, go into your room and shut the door and pray to your Father who is in secret: and your Father who sees in secret will reward you" (Matthew 6:6). The picturesque detail about shutting the door, as well as the context, provides the necessary clue for interpreting this explicit instruction about the place of prayer. It is best for us to be alone when we are privately talking with our Father. (Corporate prayer is another matter.) It may of course, be impossible to be alone in the house, if "your room" is shared with others. It was rarely possible for Jesus Himself as an itinerant teacher and healer. That is probably why we read of Him going out of the house, to pray in a solitary place (Mark 1:35). As He retired to the lonely spot, the hillside, the desert, the garden, so we may be able, sometimes, to do the same. Those situations in which we cannot ever get alone—on board ship, in the barracks, in the school dormitory—are admittedly difficult testing-times. But when we cannot do a thing, desirable in itself, God makes it up to us in some mysterious way. We are given special grace to pray where we must.

The bedroom, for most of us, most of the time, will be the normal place of prayer. It may be helpful to have a special prayer-corner in it. Leaning against the pillow, with its powerful suggestion of sleep, may not be the best place to pray! A small table, where we can sit or kneel is a help. On the table keep your Bible, and your own study and devotional books.

Richard Baxter said "Concerning the fittest place for heavenly meditation, it is sufficient to say that the most convenient is some private retirement. Therefore withdraw thyself from all society, even the society of godly men, that thou mayest awhile enjoy the society of the Lord."

Remember that:

1. We need to keep special times for prayer each day to enjoy continued fellowship with God.

2. In doing this, we are following the example of Jesus Christ.

3. In our busy modern world, we shall only *have* time if we *make* time for prayer.

4. It is best to set aside some time each morning and each evening for fellowship with God.

5. Each person must decide for himself where the morning and evening Quiet Times best fit into the pattern of the day, and the amount of time to be given to them.

6. The right place for private prayer is alone in a quiet room.

READING
THE BIBLE

We have decided to meet daily with God, to have a
Quiet Time in the morning and evening of each
day. How can we best use our time? What should
we do during that ten to thirty minutes set aside
for communion with the Lord? There are two main
elements in a Quiet Time. The devotional reading
of the Bible, and the opening up of our hearts as
we talk with God.

The purpose of Bible reading

Why should the Bible be read during the period set
apart for prayer? We need to make a distinction
between Bible *study* and the *devotional reading* of
the Bible. We study the Bible to get acquainted
with its background, contents, and message. But
this is not why the Bible should be read during a
Quiet Time. For then we have an appointment
with "the Lord and King of Scripture." We read
the Bible devotionally in order to meet with God,
and to listen to Him speaking through His word.

The primary purpose is not to learn something about or from a book, but to meet with a Person, to encounter the eternal God who is revealed in His living Word, Jesus Christ our Lord. For He is the Word of God, pointed to in the Old Testament, revealed in the New. To borrow an illustration from Martin Luther, Christ in scripture is like a baby in a crib. We go to the crib for the sake of the one who is in it. Otherwise we deserve Christ's rebuke to the Bible students of His day: "You search the scriptures, because you think that in them you have eternal life; and it is they that bear witness to me; yet you refuse to come to me that you may have life" (John 5:39, 40). To draw near to the Lord, to meet with Him, to listen to Him through His word—that is why we need to read the Bible during prayer time.

How God speaks

When God called Samuel in the temple at Shiloh, he responded "Speak, for Thy servant hears" (I Samuel 3:10). That is the attitude in which to approach the Bible reading, with listening ears and spirit sensitive to what God has to say. But what is meant by saying that God "speaks" through the Bible? Do we hear a voice addressing us in Hebrew, Greek, English, or some other language? Take the analogy of a personal letter, received in the mail from a close friend. Through the written letter the friend may reveal his mind and purpose, he may convey a message or make a request, he may rebuke or encourage, ask questions or give directions, or talk about his activities. Someone seeing you reading such a letter might well ask "What does your friend say?" *Say!* He speaks through the written word. You can hear his voice as you read his sentences. "The Bible is a letter from God, with my personal address on it." Through the written word, His word, the Lord is active, revealing His nature and purpose, and challenging, encouraging and comforting, strengthening and directing us. All devout readers of the Bible know from experience what happens, however difficult it may be to find words which adequately express it. You read a passage, and something "strikes" you, "finds" you, "comes alive" to you, "speaks" to your condition. "I felt that it had been written just for me." We are addressed by a Person through the words of a book.

How to read the Bible

In general how should we decide what part of the Bible to read during the Quiet Time?

It is better to read little rather than too much. The length of the passage to be read will depend on the time available. But it is better to think deeply on a little than to skim superficially over a lot. One story, one paragraph, one unit of material should be enough. There is no particular virtue in reading one whole chapter at a time. The chapter and verse divisions were not inserted until the Middle Ages, and they are not always in the best places! A good

Bible reader is not like a swallow skimming over the surface of a pond, but like a miner digging carefully for hidden gold. Read a little, and read it well.

Read progressively through one selected book of the Bible. The Bible is not made up of isolated texts and disconnected passages. Each book is a unity. We are to hear the message of the whole as well as of its parts.

How should the books of the Bible themselves be selected for reading? Is there any priority? Should the beginner start with Genesis and plod right through to The Revelation? It is often better to *begin with the New Testament, and by reading the Gospels.* A sound knowledge of the life, teaching, death, and resurrection of Christ, is essential to an understanding of the rest of the New Testament; and it is more meaningful to read the Old Testament in the light of its fulfillment in the New. There is also much to be said for reading together books of the same type—the Law books, the History books, the Wisdom literature, the Hebrew Prophets, the Epistles of Paul, the Gospel and Epistles of John; or books with similar themes like Leviticus and Hebrews, Daniel and The Revelation.

In reading the Bible devotionally, we should not hesitate to *skip unsuitable passages.* Why read through the nine chapters of names with which the First Book of Chronicles opens? Why read all the detailed regulations for animal sacrifice in the Book of Leviticus, or the many chapters in the

Book of Joshua which describe how the land was divided among the Hebrew tribes? This is not to question the inspiration and authority of the *whole* Bible, for God uses it in many other ways than the one we are now considering. But do not wade through passages just for the sake of saying that you have read every word. Just as some parts of the Bible are not read in public worship, so some parts are unsuitable for private devotional reading. Passages obviously unsuitable *for this special purpose* are best omitted.

There are certain books or parts of the Bible which you may need help in understanding. Much of the Bible speaks directly to the ordinary man and woman; but there are other parts which may be virtually meaningless. Unaided, he will be able to make little of the Book of Nahum, the night visions of Zechariah, the theology of the Epistle to the Romans, or the symbolism of Daniel and the Revelation. Many people start off with some difficult book and subsequently give up reading the Bible because they just cannot understand it. But why read it, or at least why read these more difficult parts, unaided?

Bible-reading notes
Guided by the Holy Spirit, Philip the evangelist overtook an Ethiopian eunuch who was reading the Book of Isaiah in his chariot, and asked him the question "Do you understand what you are reading?" The Ethiopian replied "How can I, unless

someone guides me?" (Acts 8:30, 31). God then spoke to the eunuch through the written word *interpreted* by Philip.

There is much that we may not understand in the Bible, but God has provided interpreters. The book and the fellowship, Bible and Church, belong together, and the Lord has set within the Church preachers and teachers, commentators and writers, scholars and interpreters. We can take these with us into our Quiet Times, with the expositions or notes they have written. Why read the difficult parts of the Bible without clues, when clues have been provided? The best method of Bible reading for most of us may be the use of some system of daily readings with explanatory notes and devotional aids. The best known in this country is the Scripture Union[1] which provides notes for different age groups, and for simple or more advanced study. It is true, of course, that the more we hear or read the Bible interpreted by others, the less we need aids of this kind. Insights once gained remain, if applied in daily life; our knowledge of the word grows. But for the learner, the best rule is—have your eyes on the book and your ears open to Philip and the Holy Spirit.

How to read a daily portion
You are reading the Bible in order to draw near to the Lord and listen to His word; come *with reverence and expectancy*. Ask the Holy Spirit who inspired the word, to come and illuminate you. Pray

in your own words, or you may wish to use the following scriptures: "Speak, Lord, for Thy servant heareth." "Open my eyes, that I may behold wondrous things out of Thy law."

Then *read through the selected passage slowly.* Skimming through hurriedly is of very little value. In the Book of Job it is said of the miner deep down within the earth "his eye sees every precious thing" (28:10). Reading the Bible is like mining; we have to dig deep down to find the hidden treasure. This takes time, and our reading should therefore be concentrated and thorough.

Make full use of your intellect to understand the passage. Ask yourself all kinds of questions about it. What—when—why—how—who? What is the main point, the principle truth in this story, incident, or parable? What does it teach me about God, about other people, about life, about myself? Do I understand the meaning of all the words used? Do other passages in the Bible shed any further light on it? After having thought out the meaning fully for yourself, then, if you are using a system of notes, read the notes for additional light on the passage. Do this *after* your own thinking, lest the insights of others become a substitute for your own discovery.

If you are reading a story, *use your imagination to picture the whole scene.* "Open my eyes, that I may behold wondrous things"—this can be true in a special sense of the imagination. Visualize the scene, and see "in your mind's eye" all the characters playing their parts as in a drama. Even when a reading is not story or incident, its truth can often be "seen." For example, how many pictures do you see in Matthew 7? The Bible is an art gallery; its language is concrete, vivid, picturesque. You can *see* as well as hear the word of God.

After the intellect and the imagination—the will; after the mind and the eyes, the hands, *the practical out-working or application.* What is the Lord saying to me through the written word, with reference to my own life and situation? What must I be, or do or say, as a result of this reading? For we hear the word of God in order that we may do it (Matthew 7:24). In education, the importance of what is called "expression work" is now widely recognized. We retain what we have heard and seen by doing it. For the Psalmist, God's word is not only for the ears and the eyes. "Thy word is a lamp to my feet and a light to my path" (Psalm 119:105). Let us live it out.

Remember that:
1. We read the Bible at prayer-time in order to meet with God and listen to His word.
2. The Bible is like a letter from a friend; God uses the written word to communicate personal messages and convictions to me as I read.
3. How should the Bible be read? Read a little thoroughly—read through one selected book—read the New Testament before the Old—omit passages unsuitable for devotional reading—use notes for the interpretation of difficult parts.

4. God has men within the Church who can help us understand the Bible; we accept their help by making use of Bible-reading notes.

5. How should I read the daily portion? Pray for help—read the passage slowly—think deeply about it—picture the scene—apply it to my life.

Note

[1] For information write: The Scripture Union, 38 Garrett Road, Upper Darby, Pa. 19082, U.S.A. or The Scripture Union, 3 Rowanwood Ave., Toronto 5, Ontario, Canada.

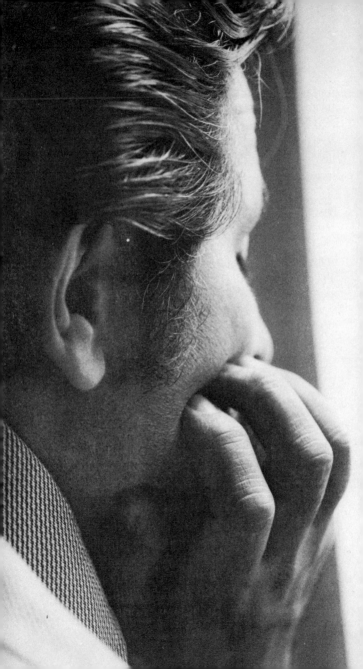

WHAT DO I
PRAY ABOUT?

5

What do I say to God?

Prayer is conversation with God; but conversation itself is a dialog, not a monolog. It is two-way traffic; it involves both listening and speaking. In the last chapter we were concerned with the listening. Through the devotional reading of the Bible, we listen to God speaking through the written word. We turn now to the other side of Quiet Time communion—speaking to God in prayer. And we shall first of all consider what is to many people the most difficult problem of the prayer life—the *content* of our prayers. The difficulty may be expressed like this. "What should I pray about? My trouble is, when I get on my knees, I just don't know what to say. So I find myself saying the same things over and over again, using clichés and threadbare sentences, offering the same few petitions, until the whole thing becomes thoroughly stale, dull, and unreal." In this chapter, four ways of filling out and varying our prayers will be described.

Take your Bible reading into your prayers

Normally in a Quiet Time, the devotional reading of the Bible should precede the main time of prayer. We should listen to God before speaking to Him. In normal conversation what I say to the other person bears some relationship to what he has just said to me. If God has spoken to me through the reading of His word, my reply to Him in prayer should be a response. Prayer is man's response to God's revelation, the human answer to Him who reveals and communicates Himself. This means that what has been read in the Bible will enter into the prayers that follow.

It is likely that the Bible reading as a whole will suggest several subjects for prayer—for thanksgiving and confession, for personal petition and intercession. Suppose, for example, that you have been reading and thinking about the story of Christ stilling the storm on the Sea of Galilee (Mark 4:35-41). As a result of the reading you may be led by the Holy Spirit to give thanks for Christ's faith, courage, and serenity; to confess your own cowardice in the face of trial and danger; to ask for yourself the faith of which Christ speaks; and to intercede for those in difficult circumstances. There are few Bible passages which do not suggest some subject for prayer. In the last section of the previous chapter—"How to read the daily portion"—a certain sequence was suggested; after thought and imagination, application. How am I to *do* the truth, how am I to express this in my life? These insights, directions, resolutions, should be turned into prayers. We ask God for wisdom, guidance, and strength to do what we have heard in His word. Since God Himself, His nature and purpose, is revealed in the Scriptures, it will be prayer in harmony with His character and will, prayer "in His Name".

Take the coming day into your prayers

If the Bible is the Christian's prayer-book, so also is daily life. Each separate day may be likened to the page of a book; as we read that page and meditate on it, the Holy Spirit will compel us to specific prayer. At the time of morning prayer, it is a good thing to look ahead, to anticipate as far as possible the coming day. Not that the events of each day can be exactly foreseen, for there is always the unknown, the unpredictable element in life. There are the surprises, painful or joyful, the sudden temptations or opportunities. On the other hand, most of the events of an ordinary day can be foreseen, and we may pray over them ahead of time. Ask yourself three questions: "*Who* will I be meeting today? *Where* will I be going today? *What* will I be doing today?" The answers to these three questions will remind you of people, situations, assignments about which you ought to pray. One of the lessons we learn from the example of Jesus Christ, is to pray about things in advance. Before He chose the twelve men who were to be the nucleus of the Church, He spent all the previous night in prayer to

God (Luke 6:12). Later on, He prayed before asking those same Apostles the great question "Who do you say that I am?" (Luke 9:20). He anticipated the last and greatest day of His life on earth with prayer (Luke 22:39-46). This last reference is doubly instructive. The Apostles who were told to pray in Gethsemane, and failed to do so, were unprepared when the crisis came. The Master who prayed was ready for anything, and completely victorious. It can make all the difference to our day if we pray about it in advance, bringing the people we are likely to meet, the task to be done, and the decisions to be made, to God in prayer.

Take the past day into your prayers

During the evening Quiet Time, we look back over our day, quietly reviewing its events in the presence of God. Three direct questions will provide subjects for confession, for intercession, and for thanksgiving. "What wrong have I done today, or what good have I left undone?" Examine your heart, confess your sins of commission and omission, and ask for forgiveness. "Of the people I have met or heard about today, do any need my prayers?" Then pray for each person in terms of his need. "What joys, gifts, mercies, blessings, have I received today?" Express your gratitude to God for each one of them. The essential thing is to bring each day to God. The manna in the wilderness, God's own provision for His pilgrim people, had to be gathered *every day*. It could not be gathered and stored up for future use (Exodus 16:13-21).

Put your desires in your prayers

One of the best definitions of prayer is to be found in the first two lines of a hymn by James Montgomery.

> Prayer is the soul's sincere desire,
> Uttered or unexpressed.

Prayer is desire. The desire may be expressed in words—our prayers—or it may be too deep for words. Here we come upon the real distinction between praying and merely saying prayers. Real prayers, whether extempore or liturgical, are the expression in words of the desires of those who are speaking them. Prayer without desire is "vain repetition," a matter of empty words. But God does not listen to polite speeches; He hears those prayers which articulate the real desires of the heart.

It is just because we often fail here that prayer seems unreal. It is insincere because we are not bringing to God our true interests, concerns, and desires. A young man of twenty is keenly interested in engineering—his job, in football—his recreation, and of course in Mary—his fiancee, whom he hopes to marry in the spring. But none of these interests is brought into his prayers because, he supposes, they are not "religious." He always prays about churches and ministers, missionaries and the sick, in none of which (unfortunately) he is particularly interested. He wonders why prayer is so dull and unreal, and is tempted to give it up. He must be helped to realize that religious experience is not a special kind of experience, fenced off from life; it is ordinary experience seen in depth, in relationship to God. He must be encouraged to pray about his real interests, to express his deepest desires in prayer, whatever they may be. All that has been said in this and in the two preceding sections of this chapter may be summed up: *bring your life into your prayers*—your daily life, work, relationships, concerns, interests, and desires. We cannot live one way and pray another. Great praying presupposes great living. Prayer and life must be joined in one.

Remember that:

1. Pray about your Bible reading. Let the passage as a whole suggest topics for prayer, and pray about the practical directions and resolutions which are the outcome of your meditation on it.

2. Pray about the coming day—the people you are to meet, the events and situations you can foresee, the work you have to do.

3. Pray about the past day—confessing sins, interceding for people in need, giving thanks for help.

4. Pray about your sincere desires and vital interests.

PRAYER PATTERNS

Prayer—planned or spontaneous?

Should a Quiet Time be planned? Should there be an order or sequence in the offering of our prayers? Or is it better to forget about a pattern, and give spontaneous expression in prayer to whatever thoughts and desires enter our minds?

We are familiar nowadays with the difference between a planned and an unplanned city. In former times, many of our towns just grew higgle-dy-piggledy, a jumble of unplanned streets. In pleasing contrast is the modern town or suburb, with industrial and residential areas, central stores and public buildings, form and beauty. Obviously a town functions better when it is planned. On the other hand, there are aspects of life which cannot be planned. It is hardly possible and it is certainly not desirable to plan a romance or a friendship; spontaneity is the essence of it. Between these extremes are other spheres of life where both planning and spontaneity are valuable. A vacation needs some planning—but not too much, for without freedom to follow the inclinations of the moment, it would hardly be a vacation.

What about prayer? Should it be planned or spontaneous—or both? There are those who believe that prayer, public as well as private, should be unplanned. It should be as free as the wind, extempore, a manifestation of the "inspired spontaneity" of the Holy Spirit. To them, to plan prayer is to quench the Spirit. At the other extreme are those for whom private prayer is largely a repetition of prayerbook phrases and public prayer a fixed liturgy. Rarely do we find these extremes in practice; it is more a matter of degree and emphasis. But it would seem that private or public prayer is at its best when there is a combination of planning and freedom, of order and spontaneity. There should be a flexible pattern which allows ample room for the free movement of the Spirit: the Spirit of order and of liberty. In this chapter we will study the principles underlying the formation of such a pattern, and some suggested outlines for the Quiet Time.

The pattern prayer

"He was praying in a certain place, and when he ceased, one of his disciples said to him, 'Lord, teach us to pray, as John taught his disciples' " (Luke 11:1). In response to this request, the Lord Jesus gave to His disciples the pattern or model prayer. It is found in Luke 11:2-4 and also in

Matthew 6:9-13. The prayer consists of an address and six petitions—the doxology is not part of the original prayer, but was added later. This is the Lord's Prayer, the perfect pattern He gave to instruct and guide His disciples. What may we learn from it?

God Himself should come first, and be the center of all our prayers. Of the six petitions, the first three have to do with God. Trusting in His love, submitting to His authority, conscious of His greatness, we address Him as "our Father who is in heaven." We pray about His name, asking that we may respect His character, and worship His revealed nature. We pray about His kingdom, asking that God will come to reign in power and love over all His creatures. We pray about His will, asking that we and all who live on this earth may obey Him, as He is already obeyed in heaven. Here Jesus Christ is saying "In your prayers, put God first, give Him the supreme place, desire His glory above all." Only when God is put first can we rightly pray for others and present our own personal requests. This means that praise, adoration and thanksgiving will have priority and prominence in the Christian's prayers.

We should be concerned with the needs of others as well as with our own basic needs. The second part of the pattern prayer is concerned with the needs of man. It consists of three petitions: for daily food (that nourishment of body and spirit without which we cannot live), for forgiveness of our sins in proportion to our own forgiveness of those who have sinned against us, that we may not be exposed to temptation (but since we cannot always avoid it, we ask for God's strength to overcome evil). Here Jesus Christ teaches us to bring our essential needs to God. So often we are concerned with what we want (which is really secondary). My basic needs are food, forgiveness and moral strength. But it is not just for my own basic needs that I am to pray. This is a *family prayer,* addressed not to "my Father" but to "*our* Father." I am taught to pray "give *us* . . . bread, forgive *us* our trespasses, deliver *us* from evil." I am to be concerned about the basic needs of the whole body of Christ, of which I am only one small part.

In the first part of the Lord's Prayer we are obeying the great commandment: "The Lord our God, the Lord is one; and you shall love the Lord your God with all your heart, and with all your soul, and with all your mind, and with all your strength" (Mark 12:29, 30). In the second part of the Lord's Prayer, we are obeying the second commandment of Christ: "You shall love your neighbor as yourself" (Mark 12:31). *As yourself—there is a right kind of self-love.* He who is as concerned for the needs of others as for his own, will be rightly concerned with his own needs.

Here then we have the true pattern, the right order for prayer—God, others, myself. The pattern of the Quiet Time should reflect this essential order. *God first*—adoration, submission to His will revealed in Scripture, thanksgiving; *neighbor second*—intercession; *myself last*—personal petition.

The pattern of listening and speaking

So far we have seen that our prayers should reflect the structure, the true order of life—God, others, myself. But there is another pattern to be thought of. As stated earlier, communion with God is a dialog, a two-way conversation. There is a rhythm of revelation and response, of divine word and human answer, of listening and speaking. Because the divine word must come before the human response, the Quiet Time should follow this pattern—listening, then speaking. A Quiet Time implies a listening. After this, we respond to God's word by speaking to Him in prayer. It is always helpful to keep this rhythm in mind when planning a Quiet Time. It is a common mistake to rush into God's presence and start talking—and to keep on talking.

"You have two ears and one mouth; so listen twice as much as you speak." This is a good rule for life, and an excellent rule for our devotions: listen, listen, speak.

Balanced prayer

Water is not an element but a compound, made up of hydrogen and oxygen. Prayer, too, is a compound of adoration, thanksgiving, repentance, intercession, petition. If the prayer life is to be whole, complete, balanced, all these different kinds of prayer must be included. It becomes unbalanced if one is omitted, or if the part is mistaken for the whole. For example, many people assume that prayer is just asking for things for themselves. But when prayer is petition and nothing else, it almost inevitably becomes self-centered. Seeing this, others have gone to the other extreme; they have dropped petition in favor of adoration, seeking God for His own sake alone. Some are given to excessive self-examination; they are always probing their souls and dwelling on their sins, real and imaginary. They would be better employed praising God and giving thanks to Him for all His goodness. Many are spiritually unhealthy for the opposite reason; they rarely examine their hearts and confess their sins.

We hear a good deal about the importance of a balanced diet. And it is needed in the prayer life. Not that every kind of prayer should be offered in every Quiet Time; but they should all have some place in my devotional life. It is helpful sometimes to devote a whole Quiet Time to just one of the five main aspects of prayer. For example, it is appropriate at the end of the week to make a full self-examination, followed by confession and a prayer for forgiveness. Make your own patterns of prayer and vary them from time to time. Here are four examples.

Outlines of prayer
Morning Prayer

Prayer for illumination of the Scriptures
Scripture reading and meditation
Prayer arising from Scripture
Prayer for the coming day
Act of surrender

Evening Prayer
Quiet review of the past day
Repentance (confession of sin or negligence today)
Intercession (for those you have met or those in need)
Thanksgiving (for the joys, gifts, and blessings of today)

Morning Prayer
Adoration (A Psalm or a hymn)
Thanksgiving
Petitions for today
The Lord's Prayer

Evening Prayer
Confession of sin
Scripture reading and meditation
Intercession
Personal submission to God

Remember that:

1. In private prayer, planning and freedom, order and spontaneity should be combined. Have a flexible plan for the Quiet Time.

2. In the Lord's Prayer, Jesus Christ taught us to

put God first, and to be concerned about the needs of others, as well as our own. The pattern is God—neighbor—myself.

3. Communion with God has the two aspects of listening and speaking. In the first part of a Quiet Time, we listen to God through His word; our prayers are a response to this.

4. There are five main kinds of prayer—adoration, thanksgiving, repentance, intercession and petition. They must all be included in the pattern for prayer.

ADORING AND THANKING GOD

7

When a white ray of sunlight is passed through a triangular glass prism, it is broken up into all the colors of the spectrum, from red to violet. Like that single ray of light, prayer can be analyzed by the mind into several parts. The most important are adoration, thanksgiving, repentance, petition, and intercession. We begin in this chapter with adoration and thanksgiving.

Adoration
Adoration is loving God for who He is. It is love looking up, like Mary of Bethany sitting at the feet of Jesus; it is love poured out, as when she anointed His feet with the precious perfume. The Scotch catechism says that "the chief end of man is to glorify God and enjoy Him forever." Man was created to adore, to express enthusiastic admiration, to acknowledge the supreme worth of God. We often come to God because we are in need of forgiveness, or of help or deliverance. We love God

because we need Him, and for dependent creatures
this is right. But although we are never without
need, and we glorify God by bringing our need to
Him, yet we can also come to God to appreciate
His greatness and to give Him our praise.

"We praise thee, we bless thee, we worship thee,
we glorify thee, *we give thanks to thee for thy
great glory,* O Lord God, heavenly King, God the
Father Almighty."

In the spring, a cherry tree in full blossom wakes
our spontaneous admiration and delight. Quite
apart from the fruit it may bear later, we enjoy its
beauty, what it is in itself. We appreciate and love
our friends not because they may help us, but for
who they are. When Isaiah "saw the Lord sitting
upon a throne, high and lifted up," he heard the
song of the seraphim: "Holy, holy, holy is the Lord
of hosts; the whole earth is full of His glory"
(Isaiah 6:3). It is this, the highest form of prayer,
the chief end of human existence, the very life of
heaven, which led Von Hugel to say "religion is
adoration."

Expressing adoration
Just because adoration is the highest form of
prayer, it is, for most of us, the most difficult.
That is not a valid reason for neglecting it until we
reach spiritual maturity. Just as human love grows
as we express it, so we learn to adore by adoring.
In the Lord's Prayer, Jesus taught us to begin with
the adoration of God. It is fitting that a Quiet

Time should often begin in this way. Here are some ways of expressing adoration.

Adore with your body; kneel down and bow your head. Lift your hands high. Your body is a part of you; what you do with it has a reflex action on your mind and spirit. "O come, let us worship and *bow* down, let us *kneel* before the Lord our Maker" (Psalm 95:6). "*Lift up your hands* to the holy place and bless the Lord!" (Psalm 134:2). The Psalmist invites us to let our bodies also participate in the worship of God. This is especially helpful on those occasions when we are not "in the mood," and do not feel like prayer. Adoration may and often does involve the emotions; but it is also a matter of attitude, intellect, intention and will. All this can be expressed in the posture of the body. To kneel, to bow the head, with the intention of expressing submission, reverence, and joy, is adoration.

Think about God and then adore Him in your own words. Call to mind some truth about Him or meditate on one of His attributes—His wisdom, power, holiness, beauty, goodness, truth. Consider Jesus—an aspect of His character, an incident from His life. After thinking for a few moments about God, express your thoughts in words of love and praise.

Use the words of others to adore God. Our own words may not seem enough. But the Scripture is full of words of prayer and praise which we may make our own. Commit some of these to memory;

then they are always available for use. Don't forget that Psalms and hymns are two great aids to adoration. "In psalms and hymns and spiritual songs, singing and making melody to the Lord with all your heart." (Eph. 5:19)

Thanksgiving

Thanksgiving is the grateful acknowledgement of God's gifts. We adore Him for who He is; we give thanks to Him for what He gives. Or do we? One of the worst features of human nature is the tendency to take things for granted. We are all guilty of receiving God's gifts without acknowledgement and gratitude, and He could complain of each one of us "how sharper than a serpent's tooth it is, to have a thankless child." When Christ healed ten lepers "One of them, when he saw that he was healed, turned back, praising God with a loud voice; and he fell on his face at Jesus' feet, giving Him thanks" (Luke 17:15, 16). If the other nine were grateful for the gift of health, they did not take the trouble to express it. We are often exhorted in the Bible to remember what God has done for us. "Bless the Lord, O my soul; and all that is within me, bless His holy name! Bless the Lord, O my soul, and forget not all His benefits" (Psalm 103:1, 2).

There are three truths about thanksgiving which it is helpful to keep in mind.

First, it is not enough to give thanks in general for all the gifts of God; it should be done in particular, in detail. Deliberately recall gifts, experiences, benefits, joys, and then give thanks for this and this and that. The advice of the old hymn is sound: "Count your many blessings, name them *one by one*; and it will surprise you what the Lord has done." One excellent way of doing this is to review the past day during the evening Quiet Time. Recall all the good things you have received during that one day, and then thank God for each one of them. At morning prayer thank God for all the gifts of the previous day, the mercies of the past night, the expected blessings of the coming day. Morning and evening—for "it is good to give thanks to the Lord, to sing praises to Thy name, O Most High; to declare Thy steadfast love in the morning, and Thy faithfulness by night" (Psalm 92:1, 2).

Second, give thanks for everything! Our natural tendency is to be grateful only for the pleasures and joys of life. Paul writes, "give thanks in *all* circumstances; for this is the will of God in Christ Jesus for you" (I Thessalonians 5:18). When he and Silas, having been flogged, were put into the inner prison at Philippi, at midnight they sang hymns to God. The gratitude of the true Christian does not depend on favorable circumstances, for "we know that *in everything* God works for good with those who love Him, who are called according to His purpose" (Romans 8:28). It is not easy, but it is wonderfully possible to thank God for trials and disappointments, for hardships and sufferings. Accept life as a whole with gratitude, knowing that everything can be used or transformed by the power of God.

Two happy results of thanksgiving may be mentioned here, by way of encouragement. When a gift of God is received by man with thanksgiving, it is consecrated, it becomes holy to the Lord. Take, for example, the habit of "saying grace" before meals. "Everything created by God is good and nothing is to be rejected if it is received with thanksgiving; for then it is consecrated by the word of God and prayer" (I Timothy 4:4, 5). This is also one of the open secrets of happiness. True, we do not give thanks in order to be happy; but it is a dependable by-product. This is an age in which many people are subject to depression. The cure is to establish the habit of daily thanksgiving.

Third, express your thanksgiving aloud. The spirit of praise is reinforced by vocal expression. An audible "Thank you, Father" in the face of joy or sorrow is a witness to God, man and Satan of our confidence that God is loving, that He is good, and that He is in control of all of our lives.

Remember that:

1. Adoration is loving, praising and enjoying God Himself.
2. Adoration may be expressed by the body; by thinking about God and putting our thoughts into words; by using Psalms, hymns and the prayers of others.
3. Thanksgiving is the grateful acknowledgement

of God's gifts, both in silent prayer and vocal expression.

4. We should give thanks not only in general, but also for specific gifts, not only for the pleasures and joys, but also for the sorrows and sufferings of life.

5. Thanksgiving has two rewards: it consecrates all God's gifts and is the surest way to happiness.

6. Thanksgiving is reinforced by being expressed *aloud*.

SELF-EXAMINATION, CONFESSION AND FORGIVENESS

The man God accepts

Christ told a story about two men who went up into the temple to pray. The one, a Pharisee, stood and congratulated himself on his many virtues and achievements. "God, I thank Thee that I am not like other men, extortioners, unjust, adulterers, or even like this tax collector. I fast twice a week, I give tithes of all that I get." The other, the tax collector "standing far off, would not even lift up his eyes to heaven, but beat his breast, saying, 'God, be merciful to me a sinner!' " Then follows the comment of Christ. "I tell you, this man went down to his house justified rather than the other; for everyone who exalts himself will be humbled, but he who humbles himself will be exalted." (Luke 18:9-14) Both men were sinful. The Pharisee was unaware of his condition; his pride was a barrier, his self-righteousness kept him from God. The tax collector was conscious of his sin and frankly acknowledged it.

We are all sinners; to know and confess this is essential if we are to approach God and be accepted by Him. In the pattern prayer, Jesus taught us to pray "forgive us our trespasses." This awareness of sin, together with the frank and sorrowful acknowledgement of it to God, is known as repentance or contrition. Repentance involves three things—facing up to our sin through self-examination, confessing it to God, and asking for and receiving His pardon.

Self-examination

"Let a man examine himself." Before I can honestly confess my sin to God, I must frankly face up to it in myself. I must look within, searching my own heart. Usually the best *time* to do this is at the beginning of the evening prayer time. Quietly review the past day in order to recall any mistakes, faults, negligence and sins within it. The end of the week, the Saturday evening Quiet Time, is also an appropriate occasion on which to make a thorough self-examination. The sins of the past week are confessed and forgiveness is received, in preparation for our worship on the Lord's Day.

Pray for the help of the Holy Spirit before self-examination. We can so easily deceive ourselves, ignoring "the weightier matters of the law" while exaggerating moral trivialities into cardinal sins. True self-knowledge is the gift of God, who alone can supply the insight, the perspective, the sincerity of purpose. It is helpful to memorize and use the following prayer from Psalm 139. "Search me, O God, and know my heart! Try me and know my thoughts! And see if there be any wicked way in me, and lead me in the way everlasting!"

Sins of omission and commission

We need to keep clearly in mind the difference between *sins of omission* and sins of commission. This distinction is well brought out in the General Confession of the *Book of Common Prayer.* "We have left undone the things that we ought to have done, and we have done the things that we ought not to have done." It does not follow that our lives are blameless because we have done nothing wrong. Having done nothing may itself be our sin. Our gravest sins are often omissions—the word of encouragement left unspoken, the opportunity missed, the work neglected, the duty shirked, the helpful deed left undone. In the parable of the Last Judgment, the wicked are condemned for their omissions. "I was hungry and you gave me no food, I was thirsty and you gave me no drink, I was a stranger and you did not welcome me, naked and you did not clothe me, sick and in prison and you did not visit me" (Matthew 25:42, 43).

Sins of commission are those of thought, word, and deed. We cannot always prevent evil *thoughts* or desires entering our minds, and being tempted is not sin in itself. But we often deliberately entertain or harbor evil in our thoughts. As for our *words,* the Apostle Paul provides us in a sentence with a dual test—"speaking the truth in love" (Ephesians 4:15). Have my words been true? Have they all been kind? And wrong *deeds,* if recent, are not hard to recall and recognize; they are obvious, concrete, definite, unmistakable. "For I know my transgressions, and my sin is ever before me" (Psalm 51:3). We will not need to probe for evil deeds; but we do need to confess those which come almost effortlessly to mind.

Christ is our standard

There is a *positive standard* by which we can measure our lives—the teaching and deeds, the life and character of Jesus Christ. That is why reading the New Testament and the Gospels in particular gives us the background for Christian self-examination. It is the light of Christ that we best see ourselves; and that does not drive us to despair simply because we are seeing Christ in His mercy and love. For deep and thorough self-examination, it is helpful to use an incident or passage from the Gospels or Epistles as background. There are four passages in the New Testament which fit this purpose:

The two commandments of love—Mark 12:28–34.

The Beatitudes, Christ's eight-fold description of Christian character—Matthew 5:1-12.

The hymn in praise of love—I Corinthians 13.

The nine fruits of the Spirit—Galatians 5:22, 23.

The use of a positive standard, keeps us from two of the dangers of self-examination. It is easy to become introspective, to become morbidly obsessed with sin. John Bunyan recognized that one of the devices of the devil was to keep him always thinking of his sins. That is almost as bad as forgetting them! It is also easy to lose our sense of perspective "straining out a gnat and swallowing a camel." The Jews, in order to avoid ceremonial defilement, refused on Good Friday morning to enter the palace of Pilate. William Temple emphasizes the irony of this: "They were demanding the crucifixion of the Lord of Glory, but of course no one thought of that as defilement; to enter the heathen ruler's house would be defilement." If we are to keep our sense of proportion, if we are to have a sense of what is vital, we need a standard of reference. If we keep looking at Christ, we shall overcome these dangers of looking within.

Confession of sin

After self-examination, confession. Having faced up to our sin, bring it to God. The Psalmist says: "I acknowledged my sin *to thee,* and I did not hide my iniquity; I said, 'I will confess my transgressions to the Lord'; then thou didst forgive the guilt of my sin" (Psalm 32:5). Having examined yourself, lift up your heart to the Savior now interceding in heaven, and tell God all about your sin. Personal confession should be *specific and definite.* Tell God exactly what it was that you thought, said or did, or neglected to do. Not, "I have been untruthful"; but "I told Jack I had climbed the mountain, when I really turned back long before reaching the top." Not "I have neglected my duty"; but "I slept all Sunday afternoon, instead of visiting my grandfather in the hospital."

On the other hand, confession is not just the acknowledgement of sins. Our sins (in the plural) are like the surface symptoms of a disease; they are the fruit of sin. I *do* evil because I *am* evil. Real contrition, deep repentance involves this acknowledgement. My sin, as distinct from sins, lies in my pride, self-will, self-centeredness; rebellion against God, alienation from God, making myself rather than God the center of my world.

Furthermore, our sin is not only personal, it is also *corporate*. Listen to this confession of the prophet Isaiah. "Woe is me! For I am lost; for I am a man of unclean lips, and I dwell in the midst of a people of unclean lips" (Isaiah 6:5). I, unclean—my nation, unclean. We are all bound together in the bundle of life, and my own sins and sinfulness have contributed to social, national, racial sin. I am, for example, a part of that world in which there are many millions of refugees, and of hungry, starving people. This is one reason why even when confessing in private, it is sometimes better to say "we" rather than "I." "Forgive us *our* trespasses" is to be prayed by an individual in his own room (Matthew 6:6 and 9).

Conditions of forgiveness

In the moving story of the vision and call of Isaiah,

there is a three-fold sequence (Isaiah 6:1-7). "I saw the Lord"; first, the vision of God in all His majesty and holiness. "And I said, woe is me"; the confession of personal sin is the result of the vision of divine holiness. "Your guilt is taken away, your sin forgiven." Having confessed his sin, the prophet is cleansed, and hears the divine declaration of pardon. Without this action of God, man's confession would be of no value. We must ask for and accept the pardon of God.

The conditions for receiving God's pardon are clearly shown in the New Testament.

First, forgiveness is offered to all those who forgive their brothers. In the Lord's Prayer, Jesus taught us to say "forgive us our trespasses, *as we forgive* them that trespass against us." This is the only petition in the prayer which Christ singled out for comment. "For if you forgive men their trespasses, your heavenly Father also will forgive you; but if you do not forgive men their trespasses, neither will your Father forgive your trespasses" (Matthew 6:14, 15).

Second, forgiveness is offered to all those who confess their sins. "If we say we have no sin, we deceive ourselves and the truth is not in us. If we confess our sins, He is faithful and just, and will forgive our sins and cleanse us from all unrighteousness" (I John 1:8, 9).

Third, forgiveness is offered to everyone who repents. Repentance is not just remorse, it is a change of mind, an act of will; the deliberate turning from self and sin to God and goodness. "Repent therefore and *turn* again; that your sins may be blotted out" (Acts 3:19).

Finally, forgiveness is offered to all those who have faith. It can never be earned by man; is not a right we can claim from God. It is possible only through the sacrifice of Christ, who "died that we might be forgiven," and lives forever to make intercession for us. "If any one does sin, we have an advocate with the Father, Jesus Christ the righteous; and He is the expiation for our sins" (I John 2:1, 2).

Receiving God's forgiveness

It is very important that we should actually ask for and take the forgiveness of God. Having fulfilled the conditions, we can do this with assurance on the ground of His promises, not our feelings. Whether or not I feel forgiven is irrelevant. "If Thou O Lord, shouldst mark iniquities, Lord, who could stand? But there is forgiveness with Thee, that Thou mayest be feared. I wait for the Lord, my soul waits, and *in His word* I hope" (Psalm 130:3-5). You may find it helpful to receive His forgiveness by a symbolic act, such as lifting up your hands to take it.

Having received God's forgiveness, we should put the sin confessed and forgiven completely behind us. "I, I am He who blots out your transgression for my own sake, and I will not remember your sins" (Isaiah 43:25). If God no longer remembers our sins, why should we? Let the experience of Christian in *Pilgrim's Progress* be ours. "So I saw in my dream, that just as Christian came up with the cross, his burden loosed from off his shoulders, and fell from off his back, and began to tumble; and so continued to do, till it came to the mouth of the sepulchre, where it fell in, *and I saw it no more.*"

Remember that:

1. God rejects the proud and accepts the repentant.

2. Repentance means facing up to sin through self-examination, confessing it to God, and asking His forgiveness for it.

3. The best time for self-examination, which should be preceded by a prayer for the help of the Holy Spirit, is at the end of a day or week.

4. We should confess the good things we have neglected to do, as well as our sins of thought, word and deed.

5. Christ is the standard by which we should examine our lives.

6. Our confession, whether of sins or of sin, should be both particular and general, personal and corporate.

7. There are four conditions for receiving God's forgiveness: the forgiveness of others, the confession of sin, repentance toward God and faith in the Lord Jesus Christ.

8. God's forgiveness should be received with confidence on the ground of His promises.

WHAT CAN
I ASK GOD?

An illuminating way of understanding God is to
think of Him in terms of the best and highest in
our human relationships. We must not be misled by
the analogy. God is unlike as well as like us. Yet in
spite of this, Christ Himself taught us to think of
prayer as analogous to the relationship between a
father and his children. An essential element in
such a relationship is *asking*. Children ask for
things; even imperfect parents respond by giving
good things. "What man of you, if his son asks him
for bread, will give him a stone? Or if he asks for a
fish, will give him a serpent? If you then, who are
evil, know how to give good gifts to your children,
how much more will your Father who is in heaven
give good things to those who ask Him?" (Matthew
7:9-11).

Prayers of asking

Prayer in which we ask God for something is called
petition. There are those for whom this one color

is the whole rainbow! For them, prayer is asking God for things—just that and nothing else. Prayer is not understood as fellowship with God, a personal communion, which, like a jewel, has many facets. There is no appreciation of adoration and thanksgiving, of repentance and submission, of listening and cooperating with God. Whenever prayer is misunderstood exclusively in terms of asking, inevitably it becomes self-centered. Man tries to use God for the achievement of his own purposes. In reaction against this narrow and selfish conception of prayer, there is a tendency to swing to the other extreme of refusing to ask at all. "I will seek God solely for His own sake, that I may live in fellowship with Him, and offer Him my worship and obedience." Such a view of prayer seems, at first sight, to be more spiritual and high-minded. But for two reasons, this is not so.

If prayer at its best is fellowship with God, then we may understand it better in terms of the analogy of our relationships with one another in human life. Have we any experience of fellowship in which asking and receiving have no place at all? Would the relationship between parents and children be "higher," if asking and giving were eliminated? Is friendship selfish because one friend requests something of the other? Is it not rather enriched by the right kind of asking and receiving? Much more convincing to the Christian, however, is the example and the teaching of Jesus Himself. Jesus asked God for things, both for Himself and for others. In His preaching and parables about prayer, the element of petition is conspicuous and indeed predominant. There can be no "higher" prayer than that practiced and taught by Christ— and that includes petition. Prayer *is* fellowship with God; a fellowship of giving and receiving, of asking and taking.

The laws of prayer

"Ask, and it will be given you; seek, and you will find; knock, and it will be opened to you. For everyone who asks receives, and he who seeks finds, and to him who knocks it will be opened" (Luke 11:9, 10). Here Christ states a fundamental truth about prayer, with no reservations or qualifications. He was not like a scientist or a logician, making cool and carefully balanced factual statements about abstract truth. He taught as a poet, appealing to the imagination, presenting one truth at a time, each with full depth and force. The necessary qualifications are supplied at other times, when He is concerned with other aspects of the truth. Those who ask, receive; but they must ask in accordance with certain laws. There are necessary conditions which must be fulfilled. What are they?

Praying in harmony with the mind of Christ

Our prayers of asking, to be effective, must be offered *in Christ's name.* "Whatever you ask in My name, I will do it, that the Father may be glorified in the Son; if you ask anything in my name, I will do it" (John 14:13). This does not mean that if we tag the name of Jesus Christ on to the end of our requests and finish up all our prayers with the magic formula, "this we ask in the name of Jesus Christ our Lord," they will be granted! In the Bible "the name" means the nature; it stands for the person as revealed in his character. To pray in Christ's name is to pray in accordance with His nature and character, in harmony with His revealed will and purpose. That is why He can say: "Truly, truly, I say to you, if you ask anything of the Father, he will give it to you in my name . . . ask, and you will receive, that your joy may be full" (John 16:23, 24).

The disciples had always prayed as devout Jews. From then on they would be able to pray according to the mind of the Master. "If you abide in me, and my words abide in you, ask whatever you will, and it shall be done for you" (John 15:7). In the teaching of Christ—"my words"—we have the mind of Christ; as a result, whatever we ask is granted (see also John 15:16). This then is the basic condition for effective petition—it must be according to Christ's revealed character and purpose.

Praying with faith

And our petitions must be offered in *faith*, with confidence in His perfect wisdom, power, and love. Even human parents know how to give good gifts to their children. "How much more will your

Father in heaven, give good things to those who ask him?" (Matthew 7:11). We are to approach Him with this sure confidence, with this serene faith. Even as we pray, we believe that God is already answering. "Therefore I tell you, whatever you ask in prayer, believe that you receive it, and you will" (Mark 11:24). James, the brother of the Lord, underlines this condition for effective prayer. "Let him ask in faith, with no doubting, for he who doubts is like a wave of the sea that is driven and tossed by the wind. For that person must not suppose that a double-minded man, unstable in all his ways, will receive anything from the Lord" (James 1:6, 7).

Praying with perseverance

Our petitions must be *persistent.* To urge perseverance in prayer, Christ told two parables. A householder is in the embarrassing position of having no food to set before an unexpected guest. At midnight he goes and knocks on the door of a friend, who, being in bed with his family, is unwilling to rise, and finally give him the three loaves for which he is asking. Then follows Jesus' own comment on the situation. "I tell you, though he will not get up and give him anything because he is his friend, yet because of his importunity he will rise and give him whatever he needs" (Luke 11:5–10).

In the second parable a defenseless widow keeps coming to a judge for arbitration and justice. Having no respect for either God or man, he at first refuses to help her. Later on he says, "Because this widow bothers me, I will vindicate her, or she will wear me out by her continual coming" (Luke 18:1-8). These are not parables of comparison but of contrast. God, who is altogether *unlike* the lazy householder and the unjust judge, will certainly answer those who keep asking. Perseverance is necessary because of delay, and the purpose of delay is to strengthen faith. "Keep on asking, and it will be given you."

Praying with love

Our petitions must be offered *in love*. God will not hear the prayers of those whose relationships with their fellow-men are unjust and unloving. "When you spread forth your hands, I will hide my eyes from you; even though you make many prayers, I will not listen; your hands are full of blood. Wash yourselves; make yourselves clean; remove the evil of your doings from before my eyes; cease to do evil, learn to do good; seek justice, correct oppression; defend the fatherless, plead for the widow" (Isaiah 1:15-17). Like Isaiah and other Hebrew prophets, Christ insists upon justice, mercy, and faithfulness in our personal relationships, and condemns the hypocrisy of those who "devour widows' houses and for a pretense make long prayers" (Matthew 23:14). If I have quarrelled with my brother, or if he is justifiably offended with me, my worship is unacceptable. "First be reconciled to your brother, and then come and offer your gift" (Matthew 5:23, 24). I must feel love for all men, when I pray. "And whenever you stand praying, forgive, if you have anything against anyone; so that your Father also who is in heaven may forgive you your trespasses" (Mark 11:25). To be in right relationship with God, we must be in right relationship with men.

These, then, are the necessary conditions if we are to receive what we ask for: to pray in harmony with His mind and purpose, with faith, persistence, and charity. And we shall receive.

Petition and character

But what is the will of God for us? It is primarily that we should be like Jesus Christ in character and action. It is God's purpose that we should *be* Christ-like persons. God is not only concerned with what we *do,* but with what we *are.* As Paul expressed it: "My little children, . . . I am again in travail until Christ be formed in you!" (Galatians 4:19). It is God's purpose that we should be "conformed to the image of his Son"; prayer according to His purpose is prayer for *that*—for Christlikeness. We are encouraged to pray for "the fruits of the Spirit" which are the virtues of Christ. Our petition is that the three great Christian virtues, faith, hope, and love, may increase in us, and that we may love what God has commanded.

In our prayers for qualities of character, we must be positive, to concentrate on the virtues or graces we need. It is easy to get into the habit of praying about faults, weaknesses, and vices. "Please, Lord, help me to overcome my bad temper." In the very act of praying, I am preoccupied with my shortcoming! How much better to pray: "Please, Lord, grant to me the patience of Christ and the fruit of the Spirit which is self-control." This is one of the great advantages of reading the Bible, especially the New Testament, in my Quiet Time. Looking first at the Lord Jesus, the petitions which are suggested by the Bible reading and meditation will be for those virtues and graces which we see in Him.

The breadth of petition

If we pray with the principles of Christ in mind, wanting to be like Him in character, then we need not hesitate to pray about everything. "Have no anxiety about anything, but in *everything* by prayer and supplication with thanksgiving let your requests be made known to God" (Philippians 4:6). We need to be on guard against the tendency to divide life into the material and the spiritual, with the assumption that it is right to pray only for spiritual things. Such a division is unbiblical. God is not concerned with a special area of life labelled "spiritual" or "religious"; *He is the Lord of all life.* All that concerns us also concerns Him and may be brought to Him in prayer.

For example, to pray for money or for a car, if you are in real need of them, is just as spiritual as to pray for a friend to be saved. Nor is it right to exclude the small or the trivial, and to confine our asking to matters of great importance. We are not always in a position to say what is trivial. It does not follow that a thing is wrong because we want it. Why assume that the will of God is unpleasant! Unless our wants are clearly contrary to the will of God, they may be included in our prayers. Pray about everything that concerns you, leaving the answer with complete assurance to Him who is perfect wisdom, power, and love. The Holy Spirit within us teaches us how to pray. This is how Lady Julian of Norwich put this truth into the mouth of God:

I am the ground of thy beseeching.
First, it is My will that thou have it,
And then I make thee to will it,
And then I make thee to beseech it,
And if thou beseech it, how should it then be that
thou should not have thy beseeching?

Remember that:

1. Not all prayer is petition; but that petition is an essential part of prayer is shown in the teaching and example of Christ.

2. There are certain necessary conditions if we are to receive what we ask for.

3. Our petitions must be in harmony with the mind of Christ.

4. We must pray with confidence.

5. When faced with delay or difficulty, we must persevere.

6. When praying, we must be in right relationships with our fellowmen.

7. We should pray first for qualities of character, for the virtues of Christ.

8. All that concerns us may be included in our petitions.

10

If you had a friend, would you go to him at midnight and say to him, "Friend, lend me three loaves; for a friend of mine has arrived on a journey, and I have nothing to set before him"? Why did the householder in this familiar parable beg for the three loaves? He was not knocking for himself, he was not asking for bread to satisfy his own hunger. He kept on knocking and asking *on behalf of another,* the unexpected guest, "a friend of mine." Asking for oneself is petition; asking for another is intercession. It has been said that "the greatest thing you can do for any man is to pray for him." Why should we pray for others?

Love on its knees
Dr. H. E. Fosdick has described intercession as "love on its knees." The householder in Christ's parable was concerned that his unexpected guest should have something to eat. Concerned! If his attitude had been "I couldn't care less!" he would

not have gone hammering on the door of a neighbor at midnight, persevering until he got what his guest needed.

We shall knock on God's door, if we really care for others. Abraham kept on interceding for the wicked city of Sodom, even at the risk of presumption, only because he cared for the city, or at least for a possible nucleus of righteous people in it (Genesis 18:22 to 33). Notice also the intercession of Moses for the idolatrous Hebrews. "But now, if thou wilt forgive their sin—and if not, blot me, I pray thee, out of thy book which thou hast written" (Exodus 32:32). So great is his love for the people, that he is willing to perish with them, though innocent, rather than live without them. Such a love drove him to his knees.

The Lord Jesus when He "knew that his hour had come to depart out of this world to the Father, having loved his own who were in the world, he loved them to the end" (John 13:1). As an expression of that love, He offered up the great prayer of intercession for His friends, the most fully recorded prayer of Jesus, before laying down His life on their behalf (John 17). But He did not confine intercession to the circle of His friends. He practiced His own precept, "love your enemies and pray for those who persecute you" (Matthew 5:44). As He was being nailed to the cross, He was praying "Father, forgive them; for they know not what they do" (Luke 23:34). Love intercedes, even in extremities.

Method useless without love

We can see here the intimate relationship between prayer and life. Intercession is not primarily a matter of technique, of "know how." Methods or plans of intercession without love are about as useful as a locomotive without steam. Love is the motive, caring the incentive. The saying "he prays best who loves best" applies especially to intercession. We fail here, not just because of a lack of time or even because of intellectual difficulties about prayer. Dr. Fosdick explains: "The chief obstacles to intercession are moral. We live for what we can get; our dominant desires are selfish. The main current of our lives runs in the channel of our ambitions, and our thoughts of other people and of great causes are but occasional eddies on the surface of the stream."

Learning to intercede is learning to love. But must we wait until we love others before we start praying for them? This is a version of the old query "Which comes first, the chicken or the egg?" It is not a case of first this and then that. Love and intercession belong together. Love a person and, if you believe in prayer, you will pray for him; pray for him and you will love him more. Intercession is one way—maybe the greatest way—of obeying the commandment, "you shall love your neighbor as yourself."

Praying for people

Intercession has been described as "prayer with

names in it." Aaron the high-priest was commanded to wear a breastpiece on which were en-
graved the names of the twelve patriarchs. "So
Aaron shall bear the names of the sons of Israel in
the breastpiece of judgment upon his heart, when
he goes into the holy place, to bring them to continual remembrance before the Lord" (Exodus
28:29).

We too are to go into the presence of God bearing names. What names? Obviously it is impossible
to pray for all the individuals on earth, and hardly
possible, for most of us, to pray for the ones we
know. This is not required of us. We should pray
for the members of our own family, for personal
friends, for all who are "near and dear," for fel-
low-workers, for acquaintances who are sick or in
need. But in addition, God often gives us what the
Quakers would call "a concern." A certain person
keeps coming to mind, and we have an awareness
of special responsibility for him.

It is a good thing to make a list of all the people
for whom we ought to pray. Such a list ensures
that no one is forgotten. It should be revised from
time to time, both by the addition of new names,
and the omission of those for whom we no longer
have a special responsibility.

How to pray for a person

How should we intercede for a person? Is it enough
to say "God bless John Smith" and leave it at that?
Hardly! Don't start praying right away. Spend a

few moments thinking about John Smith, about his circumstances and needs right now! Then bring him into the presence of the Lord, just as the four men in the gospel story carried the paralytic into Jesus' presence. Then you can pray for him. Whether or not you know his needs, remember that the primary purpose of your prayer is that he should know and do the will of God, should become more like Jesus Christ, should fulfill God's purpose. Pray this for him in your own words, or by using Paul's prayer for the Christians at Ephesus.

"For John Smith, I bow my knees before thee, O Father, from whom every family in heaven and on earth is named, that according to the riches of thy glory, he may be strengthened with might through thy Spirit in the inner man, and that Christ may dwell in his heart through faith; that he, being rooted and grounded in love, may have power to comprehend with all the saints what is the breadth and length and height and depth, and to know the love of Christ which surpasses knowledge, that he may be filled with all the fullness of God."

Then pray for him specifically in terms of his needs as you are aware of them.

Praying for causes

Although we cannot possibly pray for all people *individually,* we can and ought to intercede for whole groups of people, especially for groups engaged in some special task, or "cause." Since it is not possible to pray for everything, everyday, it is helpful to make a plan of intercession. Here is one such plan for a week.

Sunday
The Church universal. My own local church. Local church officers, teachers and workers.

Monday
My family and relatives. Personal friends. All parents, children and homes.

Tuesday
Schools, colleges and universities. Teachers, speakers, writers. Scientists, artists, sportsmen and entertainers. Children's and youth work.

Wednesday
Fellow employees. Employers and employed. My trade union. Commerce and industry.

Thursday
The work of healing. Local hospitals, doctors and nurses. The sick. The needy. The bereaved.

Friday
Our country. President, Senate and Congress. Local government. The nations and U.N.

Saturday
The world mission of the church. Individual mis-

sionaries and their societies. New converts and churches. Unbelievers—those I am concerned to win.

Dangers to be avoided

Ulysses had the difficult task of sailing his ship through a narrow strait, between the twin monsters, Scylla and Charybdis. To avoid one was to be in danger of the other. In intercession the two dangers to be avoided are narrowness on one hand and vague generalities on the other. The man who prayed:

God bless me and my wife,
My son John and his wife,
Us four—no more—Amen.

was obviously guilty of narrow, confined, self-centered, or at best family-centered prayer. There are others besides family and friends who are in need of our prayers, and a Christian should have a global outlook, not a vision which sees no farther than the village pump.

But, while avoiding narrowness and a parochial outlook, intercession should not degenerate into vagueness and generalities. What does a man expect to happen when he prays "God bless China"? Such a prayer is like an unfocused lens, like an arrow shot anywhere and therefore nowhere. Intercession should be clear, focused, definite, like the request of the householder who came at midnight for the loaves. He knew exactly what he wanted, including the number—three. One way of avoiding these extremes, and of ensuring that intercession is definite in its objectives and wide in its range, is to pray both for the individual and for any group to which he belongs. While praying for your friend who has emigrated to New Zealand, pray also for the government of that land. When interceding for a missionary in Korea, include his mission society as well as the whole Church in that country. If you are praying for someone in the hospital, include the other patients and the staff of doctors and nurses.

Only those who love deeply, and who share this conviction about the power of intercession, are likely to be faithful in this costly ministry. But it is not a ministry we exercise alone. As Aaron the high-priest went into the sanctuary bearing names for intercession, so we have a great High Priest and Mediator who lives forever to make intercession for us. We come as members of His Body, of the Church which is "a royal priesthood," a community of intercessors. We are "in Christ," praying with Him for others.

Not only are we interceding with Christ our "advocate with the Father," but also with the Holy Spirit, our advocate within. "Likewise the Spirit helps us in our weakness; for we do not know how to pray as we ought, but the Spirit Himself intercedes for us with sighs too deep for words. And he who searches the hearts of men knows what is the mind of the Spirit, because the Spirit intercedes for the Saints according to the will of God" (Romans

8:26, 27). With both Christ above and the Holy Spirit within, we intercede for others.

Remember that:

1. Intercession is praying for others.

2. The incentive to intercession is love.

3. We should pray for individuals who are "near and dear" and for those for whom we feel a special concern.

4. Think first of the needs of the individual, then bring him into the presence of Christ and pray for him.

5. We should also intercede for groups and causes.

6. Avoid both narrowness and vagueness; let your intercession be comprehensive and definite.

7. We intercede with the help of Jesus Christ above and the Holy Spirit within.

The great commandment

Once, when Jesus Christ was asked which of the six hundred and thirteen commandments of the Law of Moses came first in importance, He replied: "The Lord our God, the Lord is one; and you shall love the Lord your God with all your heart, and with all your soul, and with all your mind, and with all your strength" (Mark 12:29, 30).

Misguided attempts have sometimes been made to give exact definitions of the words, heart, soul, mind, strength, as if they referred to exactly defined and different aspects of the personality. But the Hebrews thought of man as *one whole.* For example, in the Bible the word "heart" is used of the will, of the intellect and of the emotions. In citing these words, Christ is not using the exact language of a psychologist, but the picture language of a poet. In the words of today He is saying: You shall love the Lord your God lock, stock, and barrel—hook, line, and sinker! Man is to love

God *with his whole being*. Every facet of his many-sided life, every faculty of his personality is to be involved in worship and service, trust and obedience which are God's due. And what is true of life, is true also of the devotional life.

In the last four chapters, we have been thinking about adoration, thanksgiving, repentance, petition, and intercession, stressing the fact that if the devotional life is to be balanced and whole, all these kinds of prayer must be included. But this does not of itself ensure that prayer will be full and complete. Not only every kind of prayer, but also every aspect of the personality of the one who prays should enter into the worship of God. Human beings think, feel, and will. Therefore thought, emotion, and volition should all enter fully into our prayers. Of course, these are not distinct faculties; man is not like a store with separate departments. It may be that all three—thinking, feeling, and willing—are involved in every experience, in varying degree.

It is that variation, however, which is important. In the course of one evening a teenage boy may work problems in trigonometry, listen to rock music, and wrestle with a friend. In the first, thought; in the second, emotion; in the third, striving, is predominant. In this chapter, we shall study the place of thinking, feeling, and willing, in the prayer life of the believer, as well as considering the part the body can share in the worship of God.

Mistaking the part for the whole

Life without feeling or emotion would be hardly worth living, and devotion would certainly be incomplete without it. If we are to love God wholeheartedly, our feelings must enter our worship.

But before turning to the positive aspect of this truth, we must recognize a common error. It is often assumed that because feeling is a part of prayer, we cannot pray without our feelings. It is to mistake the part for the whole. Yet this mistake is widespread, and is usually expressed like this: "I pray only when I feel like it; otherwise it would not be genuine and real." When we apply this to other aspects of life we see how absurd it is.

On Monday at 6 o'clock in the morning a busdriver is lying in bed, listening to the jarring noise of his alarm clock. He must be at work by 7:15 a.m. The morning is cold and rainy, so instead of getting up, he turns over in bed, saying to himself, "I can't go to work today, I don't feel like it"! In no sphere of life can we make the discharge of our obligations dependent on our feelings—or, if we do, it is recognized as a moral failure. To worship God is to give Him the glory *due* to His name. It is our primary obligation, to be discharged whether we feel like it or not.

Mastering our moods

Even the greatest saint does not always feel in the mood for prayer. Our feelings are changing and inconstant. This does not mean that love is inconstant, for love is not only a feeling; it is an expression of a whole relationship. The love of a good mother for her child is constant though her feelings vary with the circumstances. At one moment she feels tenderness; at another anger. Most of the time, when preoccupied with other things, she has no conscious feeling for the child at all.

So also our love for God may be constant; but within that unchanging relationship feelings come and go. To depend upon them is like building the house of prayer in a bog. For some, moods are the first great enemy of the prayer life. They can be overcome by making prayer a matter of habit, not mood; of will, not feeling. Set appointed times, established habits of prayer, and keep to them whether you feel like it or not.

Pray with your feelings if they are spontaneously present, pray without them if they are absent, pray in spite of them if they are contrary. If you hoist the sail of your prayer-boat and no wind of feeling is blowing, get out the oars of the will and row. When your prayer is a matter of will your constancy of purpose is itself a costly and precious offering to God.

Praying with our feelings

We turn now to the complementary truth. Though there can be complete devotion when feeling is absent it would, however, be far from complete if it were absent *all the time*. It is popular to disparage emotion in the religious life. A generation which has gone crazy over sport inconsistently regards enthusiasm for God as unbalanced and fanatical. To honor reason and will and despise emotion may be good stoicism; it has nothing to do with Christianity. Love is not as cold as charity! True love involves the whole personality, mind, will, and emotion. What human being would like to be the object of a love which was *always* controlled and emotionless? There is an emotional warmth and fervor in the devotion of the prophet Hosea, the apostle Paul, Bernard of Clairvaux, Charles Wesley —to mention but a few. Full devotion is suffused with emotion, and, as in human life, it gives warmth, color, and depth to the relationship with God.

Kindling the fire

There is a great need today for Paul's warning: "Do not quench the Spirit" (I Thessalonians 5:19). The worship of the primitive Church was pentecostal. The Spirit, outpoured at Pentecost "with a sudden great sound, as it had been a mighty wind, in the likeness of fiery tongues," continued to move in the assembly, and to inspire spontaneous praise, prayer, and utterance. Wind and fire! A plea has already been made for pattern and order in the devotional life. But what use is pattern without power, order without fervor? The Spirit who moves and teaches us to pray is like wind and fire. When the wind does blow, don't furl the sail; when the fire does burn, don't pour cold water on it. What is more, though we cannot directly kindle the fire, we can bring plenty of material for the burnt-offering to "the God who answers by fire" (I Kings 18:24). Singing the psalms and hymns, reading and pondering the Scriptures, speaking to the Lord freely in the joy of spontaneous prayer, we will be able to say like the men of Emmaus "Did not our hearts burn within us while he talked to us on the road, while he opened to us the Scriptures?" (Luke 24:32). Whenever the heart is "strangely warmed," whenever we are "carried away," we can well afford to leave behind our plans or orders, and go wherever the Spirit leads.

Praying with the will

We must love God with emotion, and yet the devotional life must not be based solely on emotion. Luke describes how Jesus, as His ministry moved to the climax, "steadfastly set His face to go to Jerusalem." Let us borrow that expression to describe the true basis of the devotional life. The face must be set in the direction of God. There must be the will, the steadfast intention, the strong determination to live in fellowship with God, and to give Him the glory due to His name. In practice, this means having a habit and practice of prayer, however simple or modest. By keeping to it, we are delivered from the tyranny of mood and circumstance, and reserve in our busy lives a place for the worship of God.

It is hardly possible to exaggerate the importance of good habits in prayer, as in life generally. By means of them we acquire or improve our abilities; many of our most valuable skills are due to the formation of habits. The mind is set free to attend to other matters. Best of all, we are saved from the unnecessary strain of having to make decisions about everything we do.

William James observed: "Habit is the enormous flywheel of society, its most precious conservative agent. There is no more miserable human being than one in whom nothing is habitual but indecision. Full half the time of such a man goes to the deciding, or regretting, of matters which ought to be so ingrained in him as practically not to exist for his consciousness at all." The habits of typing and of driving a car are useful, because the patterns of action no longer require the conscious attention of the mind, which is therefore set free for other activity. Going for a walk can be enjoyable because the mind is not preoccupied with the habit of walking. When prayer becomes habitual, the mind is set free in both these ways. We don't need to keep on making decisions about place, time, method, and so on. And in the act of prayer itself the mind, no longer taken up with the "how," is free to attend to God.

Praying with our minds

It has just been stated that the true function of habit in prayer is to set the mind free *to attend* to God. Habit becomes mechanical when it is made a substitute for thought and understanding. It is easily possible to say prayers, to sing psalms or hymns, to repeat the words of the liturgy, without any thought or attention at all. That is a wrong use of habit. Good habit is the servant of full attention. I can give creative thought to the manuscript I am typing because I need give so little attention to the technique of typing. "Habit and attention must therefore cooperate in the life of worship. Habit alone easily deteriorates into mechanical repetition, the resulting sin of the liturgical mind. Attention alone means, in the end, intolerable strain ... But it is the beautiful combination of order and spontaneity ... which is the mark of a genuine spiritual maturity and indeed the fine flower of a worshipping life."[1]

Attention should also be in working partnership with emotion as well as with habit. The apostle Paul did not belittle the place of emotion and ecstasy in the worship of the Church at Corinth, but he warned against worship which always left out intelligence and understanding. "If I pray in a tongue, my spirit prays but my mind is unfruitful. What am I to do? I will pray with the spirit, and I will pray with the mind also; I will sing with the spirit and I will sing with the mind also" (I Corinthians 14:14, 15). Thought, reason, intelligence, feeling, understanding are to be fully engaged in praise, prayer, and utterance. Consistent emotion without understanding becomes emotionalism and habit without understanding becomes formalism.

PUTTING MYSELF INTO MY PRAYERS   103

"You shall love the Lord your God . . . with all your mind." There are several ways of obeying this part of the great commandment in our prayers.

First, when you sing a psalm or hymn, or say a written prayer, *think of the meaning of what you are saying.* Avoid the habit of saying a familiar prayer, such as the Lord's Prayer, without any attention to the meaning. Concentrate. Mean what you say. In extempore prayer, avoid the use of meaningless clichés and sentences. Say what you mean.

Second, *give some thought to the content of your prayers* before praying. Look ahead over the coming day, or review the past day. Think before you make your confession or thanksgiving. Think of the needs of the other before you intercede, or of your own needs before offering petition. Think, then pray.

Third, let *meditation*--that is to say, disciplined and sustained thinking about God--have a place, whenever possible, in your Quiet Time. Chapter 4 has already discussed this.

Last, bring your full powers of *intelligence* to the study and practice of prayer.

Praying with our bodies

Because, as Robert Browning said, the flesh may help the soul, the body also has a part in the prayer life. Man is not pure spirit, but embodied spirit. To say that our actions are the expression of our thoughts and emotions is only half the truth. The expressive actions of the body can also quicken and strengthen thought and emotion. What happens when I see a bull in the field where I am walking? Do I run away because I am afraid, or am I afraid because I run away? Psychologists James and Lange have emphasized the truth in the second part of that question. Emotion may lead to action, but action also evokes and strengthens emotion. I feel more angry when I clench my fists and strike a blow. If I make myself smile and burst into laughter, I shall probably begin to feel cheerful. The expressive action of the body does react for good or ill on the human spirit. Love to God or man grows by means of the acts which express it. It was the denial of this truth which led Baron von Hügel to say "What a curious psychology which allows me to kiss my child because I love it but strictly forbids me to kiss it in order to love it." This principle has an important bearing on the devotional life.

Body prayers

The people of the Bible were not afraid to pray and praise with their bodies. "O come, let us worship and *bow down,* let us kneel before the Lord our Maker!" (Psalm 95:6). Jesus looked up to heaven, or knelt upon the earth when He prayed (John 17:1; Luke 22:41). The early Christians prayed "lifting holy hands" (I Timothy 2:8). It is a good thing to practice praying in any position, standing, sitting, lying, kneeling, for there may be times, such as a prolonged illness, when kneeling is not possible. But the act of kneeling can be a symbolic expression of submission and reverence to God. Many Christians have also found it helpful to fold the hands for prayer, like the Roman soldier placing his hands between those of the commander as he made his oath of allegiance. Let us use our lips to vocally express our prayers; it is more helpful than just thinking them in the mind. Prayer is conversation, and thought should be expressed in spoken word. We cannot always say our private prayers out loud, because other people may be present; but it is usually possible. To stand, to kneel, to bow, to prostrate oneself, to lift up the hands, to close the eyes or raise them to Jesus, to cover the face, to fold the hands, to speak, to sing, to raise high our Bibles—these are some of the ways in which worship can be expressed through the body.

In saying this, we have been using the word "body," of the physical frame and organism. But in the Bible, the word has a much richer connotation. It stands for the whole personality, the total man. All that is written in this chapter is therefore summed up in Paul's great appeal, "Present your bodies as a living sacrifice, holy and acceptable to God, which is your spiritual worship" (Romans 12:1).

Remember that:

1. The whole personality of man should be in-

volved and expressed in the worship of God.

2. Feeling is a part, not the whole of prayer; it is a mistake to pray only when you feel like it.

3. We can master our moods by making prayer a matter of repeated and deliberate practice.

4. Emotion gives warmth, richness and depth to the prayer life.

5. Do not stifle, but gladly accept spontaneous emotion.

6. The devotional life must be based on the will; upon a habitual prayer.

7. Habit stabilizes prayer and sets the mind free to attend to God.

8. But without thought and understanding, habit degenerates into mere routine, emotion into emotionalism.

9. There are four ways of praying fully with the mind. Think of the meaning of what you are saying; think about your prayers before you pray; let meditation have a place in the Quiet Time; study the practice of prayer.

10. The expressive actions of the body can express quicken and strengthen the inner life of devotion.

Notes

[1] *Worship*—Evelyn Underhill (Nisbet).

PRAYING TOGETHER

12

Christ prayed with others

"But when you pray, go into your room and shut the door and pray to your Father who is in secret" (Matthew 6:6). So far we have been thinking of the individual praying alone. Christ taught us to do this, and He did it Himself. Early in the morning, late in the evening, He withdrew to the solitary place, the hillside, the garden, for personal communion with God.

But this is only one aspect of His prayer life. He who prayed alone also prayed with others. It was His custom to share in the public worship of the synagog, in the praises and prayers, in the public reading and exposition of the Scriptures. Even His withdrawals were not necessarily for solitary prayer. "Now it happened that as he was praying alone the disciples were with him" (Luke 9:18). When He went up into a high mountain to pray, He took with Him Peter, James and John (Luke 9:28). These same three close friends also accompanied

Him into the Garden of Gethsemane, and they must have overheard His prayer, otherwise they could not have recorded it (Mark 14:33). In the Upper Room, Christ, on behalf of the whole company, gave thanks over the loaf and the cup (Mark 14:22, 23). On that same night when He was betrayed, "He lifted up his eyes to heaven," and in the presence of the apostles, prayed for them and for the whole Church of the future (John 17). Calvary was no solitary place; yet Jesus prayed there (Luke 23:34 and 46).

Immediately after the resurrection, the disciples were meeting for corporate prayer. It was upon a company at prayer that the Holy Spirit was poured out on the Day of Pentecost (Acts 1:14). The first converts "devoted themselves to the apostles' teaching and fellowship, to the breaking of bread and the prayers" (Acts 2:42). The Lord had prayed habitually with the apostles, and from the very beginning the apostolic Church was a community at prayer. If we are to "follow in His steps," we must pray alone and we must pray with others.

The advantages of praying with others

What are the advantages, the fruits, the blessings of praying together? The greatest is the promised *presence* of Christ. The promise of His real presence linked with a saying about prayer. "Again I say to you, if two of you agree on earth about anything they ask, it will be done for them by my Father in heaven. For where two or three are gathered in my name, there am I in the midst of them" (Matthew 18:19, 20). The Jewish rabbis used to say that when two people met to study the Law, the Shekinah, or Presence, was between them. All down the ages, Christians assembled in the unity of prayer have been aware of the unseen presence of the living Lord.

Corporate prayer also *quickens and kindles* the spirit of the individual as he shares in the common life and action. The experience of Martin Luther is typical. "At home, in my own house, there is no warmth or vigor in me, but in the church when the multitude is gathered together, a fire is kindled in my heart and it breaks its way through." Coals in the fire glow and burn brightly together; take one burning coal, place it separately on the hearth, and it is soon cold and dull. This does not mean that the devotion of an individual languishes because it is private. But it may grow cold because it is not *also* corporate. Both are necessary. We "maintain the spiritual glow" in our private prayers by praying with others, in our corporate prayers by praying privately.

There is also *a deeper joy* in praying together, an added vitality, a "plus" difficult to define. It is rather like the difference between eating your supper alone, and sharing in a feast. It is not just a matter of food, the something more is the company, the fellowship. So it is with prayer.

Lastly, praying together is the best way of *learning* how to pray. Prayer is conversation, and we converse in company. Whoever learned to talk in solitude? We learn best to converse with God in the company of those who pray to Him.

Now a prayer circle may be small or large. The number praying together may vary from the tiny cell of two or three, the larger prayer group or meeting, the local Church and the universal Church.

"Where two or three are gathered"

As Cleopas and his friend walked to Emmaus on the first Easter day, the risen Lord joined them and talked to them on the way. This can happen always, whenever two or three believers commune together. When two Christians really meet, that is, enter into deep fellowship, they always meet the third. Shouldn't there be, at an appropriate time, some recognition of this? Should not the two, like Cleopas and his friend (his wife?), stop talking with each other in order to talk with the Lord? The two may be husband and wife, praying together in the home at the beginning or the end of the day, or in times of special thankfulness or need. The two or three may be father, mother and children, praying as a family after breakfast, or at the bedside of the children at night. The two may be close friends who have spent a pleasant evening of talk and conclude by talking to God. The two or three may be Christians who, having a common concern to win others for Christ, meet to intercede. Such small prayer cells are very valuable. The private devotion of each individual is quickened and enriched. Because the two or three "agree," are in deep personal harmony, have a unity of purpose, their prayers are answered (Matthew 18:19). Mutual confidence makes it possible to pray with a fullness and intimacy not possible even in a prayer meeting. Best of all, the fellowship between the members of the cell is strengthened and fulfilled, as together they enter communion with the Lord.

The prayer group

In addition to formal corporate worship, the preaching of the word and the Lord's Supper, Christians from the beginning met for prayer. After Christ's ascension and before Pentecost, the Apostles "devoted themselves to prayer" (Acts 1:14). In the crisis of persecution, the assembled Church spontaneously burst into prayer (Acts 4:23-31). When Peter was imprisoned and threatened with execution "many were gathered together and were praying" (Acts 12:12). As for size, the prayer meeting is usually about midway between the tiny cell and the local Church. But this is not the main way in which it differs from both. The dominant purpose of a prayer meeting is intercession. The Christians had assembled in "the house of Mary, the mother of John whose other name was Mark" to pray for the release of Peter. There was a single aim—intercession.

A prayer group meets to cooperate through prayer with the purpose of God in the lives of others. This is a work, a ministry demanding the time, the interest, and the energies of those who share in it. The members of a prayer group may have their work in common—they may be teachers in a school, nurses in a hospital, the staff of a youth organization. When this is not the case, as in a Church prayer meeting, the purpose for gathering, the prayer objectives, must be set clearly before the people. Specifics are the life of a prayer meeting. There must be something as definite and urgent as the release of Peter from prison. *There always is.* It takes imagination and leadership to define it and to convey the sense of urgency. Perhaps the best kind of prayer group is the one which combines study and action with intercession. Here, the study of the Bible strengthens the faith and fellowship of those who pray for others, and go out to act on their prayers.

The purpose and pattern of worship

We come now to the best known and most important way in which Christians pray together—the corporate worship of the local church. All that was said in the first chapter about the chief purposes of prayer applies directly here. The main purpose of corporate worship, as of private prayer, is *fellowship with God.* This fellowship has two aspects, giving and receiving. This two-fold movement, this rhythm of offering and accepting underlies all that we do in worship and is the key to its meaning.

The patriarch Jacob saw in a vision a stairway

reaching up from earth to heaven. On this "ladder" there was two-way traffic. The messengers of God were ascending from Jacob to God, and descending from God to Jacob. This is a good illustration of what goes on in true worship. Like the ascending angels, our praises and prayers, our gifts and the love of our lives, go up to God and are accepted by Him. This is the approach of man to God, worship as offering. But this movement is itself a response to the descending God, who comes to His worshippers, speaks to them in scripture and preaching, and gives Himself in word and sacrament. The purpose of this two-fold movement is encounter, meeting, communion. We come to church to meet the Lord, to receive the Lord, to give ourselves to the Lord.

How to be a part of the service

Since worship is the most important thing we ever do, man's chief end, we ought to do it well. That means doing four things.

Prepare yourself thoroughly for worship. As already suggested, this preparation should begin at home. Devote the Saturday evening prayer-time to an act of self-examination and confession. Accept God's forgiveness, so that you come to worship on the Lord's Day "with a clean mind and a pure heart." The Sunday morning Quiet Time may include intercession for the ministry and the services of the day. As you enter your church building spend a few moments in prayer, asking the help of the Holy Spirit for those who lead the service, for your fellow-worshippers and for yourself. Those few moments of quiet are invaluable. Don't try to pack too much into them; relax, quieten the mind, open your heart to the presence of God.

Participate fully in the worship. A church is not a theater; you have not come to be a spectator of something done by others. You are yourself a part of the drama. Participate in the common action, the concerted movement of the whole worshipping congregation—"that *together* you may with *one* voice glorify the God and Father of our Lord Jesus Christ" (Romans 15:6). Join wholeheartedly in the worship, with all those who are present. Sing the psalms and hymns. Join in the congregational readings and responses. Don't hum and mumble—sing and say! Let the whole of you, your understanding, your emotions, your will, your body, participate. What you receive from worship depends upon what you put into it.

Listen intently to God in worship. You have come to meet with God and to hear what He has to say to you. He will speak through the reading of the scriptures and the preaching of the word. Don't come to hear a human being, or to pass judgment upon what you hear. Come to hear the Lord God, that you may obey His word. Of course we have to sift the wheat from the chaff—and sometimes there is a lot of chaff! But keep the main purpose always in mind. "Speak, Lord, for thy servant hears."

Offer yourself to God in the worship. You have

come to give; worship is offering. "Like living stones be yourselves built into a spiritual house, to be a holy priesthood, to *offer* spiritual sacrifices acceptable to God through Jesus Christ" (I Peter 2:5). Sing the psalms, hymns, anthems *to God,* as a sacrifice of praise. Offer up the prayers *to God.* Share fully in the offering. This is not just the giving of money, but that of which money is the token—our daily work. These spiritual sacrifices of praise, prayer and gift, can only be acceptable if they are all alike tokens of the giving of yourself. You have not worshipped unless you have offered yourself to God. "I appeal to you therefore, brethren, by the mercies of God, to present your bodies as a living sacrifice, holy and acceptable to God, which is your spiritual worship" (Romans 12:1).

Holy communion

In the service variously called the Breaking of Bread, the Lord's Supper, the Holy Communion, the Eucharist, the prayers of the individual and of the Church reach a climax. Instituted by the Lord Himself, this primitive Christian service, the pattern of all worship, can be the center and inspiration of all our devotion. Writing to the Philippians, Paul gives a twofold description of the worship of the New Covenant. "For we are the true circumcision, who worship by the Spirit of God, and glory in Christ Jesus" (3:3). This glorying in Christ Jesus, incarnate, crucified, risen, exalted, in the power of the Holy Spirit is the supreme purpose of the Lord's Supper. This Christ-centered service, which is both personal and corporate, something said and something done, can transform all our devotion into a glorying in Christ Jesus. We come to the Lord's Table to do five things.

Give Thanks. The Lord's Supper was called the Eucharist by the Fathers of the early church; this is the Greek word for Thanksgiving. In accordance with Jewish custom, at the Last Supper the Lord Jesus gave thanks for the loaf and the cup, thereby consecrating them to God. We give thanks for the body and the blood of Christ. By the sacrifice and victory of the cross and the resurrection, we have been redeemed from sin and death. We are grateful to Christ for what He has done and continues to be. The Eucharist is a feast, a festival of gladness, a service of triumph. Come to give thanks.

Remember. When the Lord Jesus gave thanks for the loaf He said, "This is my body which is for you. Do this in *remembrance* of me." After giving thanks for the cup He said, "This cup is the new covenant in my blood. Do this, as often as you drink it, in *remembrance* of me" (I Corinthians 11:24, 25). The English word "remembrance" translates the Greek word *anamnesis* which in Latin was rendered *memoria.* But when we speak of the Lord's Supper as a memorial, we must take care to recover the biblical meaning of the word "remembrance." Nowadays, to remember is to recall a past event or an absent person. But in the Lord's Supper, Christ is not absent but present, and His sacrifice is not only a past event, but a continuing reality. In our worship we enter the holy place, we join Christ our High Priest in heaven, where He offers Himself perpetually to the Father. Christ and His sacrifice is present, and is re-called, set forth, re-presented in the Eucharist. This is the meaning of "anamnesis." The past event, the sacrifice of the cross, is made operative in the present, as we join Christ at the heavenly altar. Come to recall.

Take. "The cup of blessing which we bless, is it not a *participation* in the blood of Christ? The bread which we break, is it not a *participation* in the body of Christ?" (I Corinthians 10:16). Here the word translated "participation" (*koinonia*) is variously rendered as fellowship, communion, sharing, partnership. "Holy Communion" means joint-participation in the body and blood of Christ. "Body" in the Bible means "personality"–the whole person; and "blood" stands for life which has been sacrificed. In the Lord's Supper, we are joint-participators in the personality of the risen Christ, in the life which has passed through death. We do not come to receive *something,* a substance; we come to receive a Person, who is mediated through the word and the fellowship, the actions and the elements. Come to receive Him.

Vow. In the Roman Empire, the word "sacrament" was used of the pledge or vow of allegiance made by the soldier, as he placed his folded hands between those of the Commander. Our vow of

loyalty to Christ made in baptism is constantly re-
newed at His Table. This is a pledge not only of
loyalty to Christ, but also to all those who share
with us in His sacrificed life. We undertake to live
in covenanted or bonded love with the members of
His Body. The holy kiss of love and peace, "the
sacrament of friendship," which was part of the
primitive rite, is a symbol of this. Come to pledge
your loyalty to Christ and His Body.

Offer. The Eucharist is a sacrifice. We offer our
praises and our prayers, the gifts of bread and
wine, with our own lives as a "reasonable, holy and
living sacrifice." All this we do in union with
Christ, whose sacrifice we show forth and re-pre-
sent, and in whom we offer ourselves to the
Father. Come to offer yourself with Christ.

The universal church

The individual, the cell, the group, the local
Church at prayer, are all part of the universal
Church, "which is the blessed company of all believers." It is never possible for us to meet and pray
with the whole Church; even the largest and most
representative gathering of Christians is but a small
fraction of it. Yet, in fact, it is never possible for
Christians to meet and pray apart from the whole
Church. My whole body acts when I turn over a
page with my little finger. The devotion of the
individual, the prayers of the two or three gathered
in Christ's name, the worship of the local Church,
each Communion Service—these are actions of the

whole Body of Christ. It is important to pray consciously and deliberately with the whole Church. It helps to remember that the Bible you read, the psalms and hymns you sing or repeat, the prayers you say, are being used by Christians all over the world. Remember that when you begin to pray, you are joining in an activity which is already going on apart from you, and which will continue when you have ceased your devotions.

It can be a great joy and satisfaction to add your own small quota to the unceasing worship of the one, holy, complete family of God. Our praise to God joins the timeless stream of praise from the company of the apostles, the goodly fellowship of the prophets, the noble army of martyrs, with a great multitude which no man can number, with angels and archangels and all the company of heaven. When you are face to face with the Father, you are with the whole family.

Remember that:

1. Christ our example, prayed with others as well as in solitude.

2. The blessings of corporate prayer are—the assurance of Christ's presence, the quickening and kindling of devotion, a deeper joy through sharing, learning in praying.

3. Christian partners and friends should pray together.

4. A prayer-group cooperates with God through intercession; it should have definite objectives and

a sense of urgency.

5. Christian worship is a two-way fellowship with God in which He speaks and gives Himself to us in word and sacrament, and we give ourselves to Him in praise, prayer, offering our money and ourselves.

6. Putting the best into a service means—careful preparation, whole-hearted participation, attentive listening, complete self-offering.

7. We do five things at the Lord's Supper—give thanks for Christ, remember Christ, receive Christ, vow allegiance to Christ, offer ourselves with Christ.

8. We should offer our prayers as part of the unceasing worship of the whole Church.

13

"Devotion is neither private nor public prayer; but prayers, whether private or public, are particular parts or instances of devotion. Devotion signifies a life given, or devoted, to God." In the opening sentence, just quoted, of that great devotional classic "A Serious Call to a Devout and Holy Life," William Law warns us against mistaking the part for the whole. Private and public prayers are necessary—but they are only "parts or instances." Devotion must include the whole of life; it *is* life devoted to God.

Walking with God

And it is by the consecration of one special part, that we are enabled to consecrate the whole. We keep the Lord's Day holy, so that all days may be sacred; the Lord's Table holy, so that all our meals may be sacraments; the Lord's House holy, so that all creation may be His temple. The special times of prayer, therefore, whether in private or in church, are not ends in themselves. They are not intended to be little islands of fellowship and peace, cut off from the great continent of ordinary life.

This truth is finely expressed in the metaphor of "walking with God," which is found in many parts of the Bible. Two people walking together have the same destination, and the joy of companionship on the way towards it. They often talk together; and it is a two-way conversation of listening and speaking. At times they neither speak nor listen, but walk along together in silent thought, yet each is fully aware of the presence of the other. So is communion with God. We have our regular times of private and public prayer, when we speak to Him, and read and listen to His word. But these special times are only *part* of our communion. We are to be with Him even when we are not speaking or listening to Him.

Taking our praying into our living

One thing we should do, is to take praying out into living. It is a mistake to confine prayer to the sacred times and places, the quiet room, the prayer-group, the church. Eliezer, the servant of Abraham, was praying as he stood by the well, with the camels kneeling, and the young girls approaching to draw water (Genesis 24:12-14). Nehemiah did not need to retire to his room to pray for guidance: there was no time for that. As he stood in the dining hall, offering the cup to the Persian

Emperor, he prayed to the God of heaven (Nehemiah 2:4). The Savior, who habitually sought the solitary place, also prayed as they were nailing His hands to the cross, in the presence of the soldiers and with the crowds standing around (Luke 23:34). Paul gave thanks for his daily food on the deck of a storm-tossed ship, in the presence of the passengers and crew (Acts 27:35). These are but a few examples, taken from the Bible, of concise prayers offered up *in the setting of events,* by men who walked with God. Usually, as with Eliezer and Nehemiah, no one need know that prayer is being offered; it often is, and sometimes is not desirable to conceal it. Why conceal the fact that you are "saying grace," just because you are eating in a public restaurant? But whether secretly or not, let us pray in life-situations, in the setting of events, so that praying and living may be one, woven together like the warp and woof of a garment.

"Arrow" prayers

"Ejaculatory," derived from the Greek word for a javelin, is the word used to describe those short, pointed, sentence-prayers of deep desire, which are aimed at God in daily life. The swift upward look of adoration and trust, when there is time for nothing more; the loving repetition of the sacred name of Jesus; the lifting up of the heart in a word of gratitude—such fleeting thoughts help to keep us in unbroken communion with God. The housewife washing up at the sink sings the verse of a familiar hymn of praise, as acceptable to God in the kitchen as in church. The sick visitor crossing the hospital lobby offers intercession for the patient about to be seen. The man waiting for an important job interview, sends up to God an "arrow prayer" for strength and guidance. The old man in his armchair by the fire confesses there and then the malicious thought he has been harboring in his mind, and asks for God's forgiveness. The father, reading an encouraging letter from his son, responds with a prayer of thanksgiving to God. Here prayer is only a word, a phrase, a sentence. It is like a telegram, conveying a significant message in a minimum of words, but those few words winged with strong desire are a communication with God.

Thinking about God

Communion with God, however, is not just a matter of words, few or many. Two friends walking together are not necessarily talking all the time. We can be aware of God's presence even where there is no message to communicate, no prayer to be uttered. Of course a Christian cannot always be thinking of his Lord. No human father would be so unreasonable as to ask his son to be always thinking about him! During most of the day, our thoughts are rightly concentrated on people, events, and the activities with which we are occupied. Dr. William Temple once said that a man driving a bus down Oxford Street, London during the rush hour, ought not to be thinking about God.

He is pleased when we attend to our work, or to the people around us, through both of which we are also dealing with Him.

We are not, then, required to think about God all the time, or even most of the time. On the other hand, when one person loves another, the recollection of the absent loved one takes place many times during the day. "For where your treasure is, there will your heart be also" (Matthew 6:21). Our thoughts wander readily in the direction of those we dearly love. So much so, that we can say with pardonable exaggeration, "You are always in my thoughts." If we love our Lord, who is not absent, though invisible, the thought of Him and of His nearness will come frequently to our minds. Of course, no one of us loves the Lord as he ought. That is why it is helpful to establish the habit of turning our thoughts to God during the odd moments of the day. For love grows by means of the acts which express it. As Brother Lawrence puts it, "We must know before we can love. In order to know God, we must often think of Him; and when we come to love Him, we shall then also think of Him often, for our heart will be with our treasure."

How to remember
"We must often think of Him." There are many practical ways of learning how to do this. One man stuck a bit of stamp-paper on the glass of his watch, to remind him of the presence of God. Many times during the course of the day he would

glance at his watch—to see if it were time to get up, time for morning coffee, time for that afternoon appointment. At every point that piece of stamp-paper would say "You are here and now in the presence of God."

Another person associates a certain street, along which he passes twice daily to and from the railway station, with the presence of God. A farmer recollects God's presence whenever he opens any of the gates on his farm. Times, places, objects, events, people, may all be associated in the mind with the thought of God's presence; and may thus be used to lead us to God, instead of taking us away from God. The Hebrews were commanded by God to wear tassels on their garments, to remind them of His commandments (Numbers 15:37-40). Of course tassels have nothing to do with commandments. The association is entirely arbitrary. Any other thing, carried about and seen constantly, would have served as well. It was a useful device, a practical aid to remembrance.

Use the odd moments

If we are to practice the presence of God in these ways, then we must learn to make good and fruitful use of the odd moments of the day. For every day has its odd moments when our minds are free. There are the times we spend cooling our heels on railway platforms, standing in check out lines or waiting at the barber's. What use do we make of the time spent on bus or train journeys, or standing on escalators? There are the little times between doing other things, the minutes we spend waiting for the unpunctual, the times of relaxation after meals—and so on. These are moments in which the mind can recollect the presence of God, and it may be, speak to Him. Brother Lawrence learned to practice the presence of God in this way, when he was serving as a soldier. "A little lifting up the heart suffices; a little remembrance of God, one act of inward worship, though upon a march, and sword in hand, are prayers which, however short, are nevertheless very acceptable to God." A person will often excuse his neglect of God by saying, "I have no time to pray." Are there then no odd moments in the life of even the most busy person? This is a way of prayer for busy people; it should not be the only way.

The rewards of recollection

The habit of recollecting God's presence during the day helps our Quiet Time, our special time of prayer. The most common, and to many the greatest difficulty encountered in prayer is that of wandering thoughts. "I just cannot concentrate. I begin to read the Bible, and my mind goes off at a tangent. I start to pray, and my thoughts wander all over the place." When that happens, there is only one thing we can do *in* a Quiet Time, and that is to keep on *recalling* our mind without fuss or worry. But there is a good deal to be done about it *outside* the Quiet Time, as Brother Lawrence had discovered. "One way to recollect the mind easily in the time of prayer, and preserve it more in tranquillity, is not to let it wander too far at other times." Can we really expect to concentrate in the quiet room or the church service, if we never bother to think about God throughout the day or the week? Recollection outside the Quiet Time ensures concentration within it. There is, however, a far greater reward, for we "establish ourselves in a sense of God's presence, by continually conversing with Him."[1] Intellectually, we may accept as true the statements of the psalmists: "Nevertheless I am continually with thee; thou dost hold my right hand (Psalm 73:23). Whither shall I go from thy Spirit? Or whither shall I flee from thy presence? If I ascend to heaven, thou art there! If I make my bed in Sheol, thou art there!" (Psalm 139:7, 8).

With our minds we may believe the Divine promises: "My presence will go with you, and I will give you rest (Exodus 33:14). Lo, I am with you always, to the close of the age." (Matthew 28:20).

But it is only by *the practice* of the presence of God, that we *realize* this truth and *appropriate* these promises in experience. Then, substituting his own personal name, a man can write his autobiography in the four words "Enoch walked with God" (Genesis 5:24).

Remember that:

1. Private and public prayer are only a part of devotion, which must include the whole of life.

2. Special prayer-times enable us to walk with God at all times.

3. Take your prayers out into your life; *pray as things happen.*

4. Quick "arrow prayers" help to keep us in touch with God throughout the day.

5. Establish the habit of recollection, of thinking about God during the course of the day.

6. Set up helpful associations, use practical aids to remind yourself of God's presence.

7. Make use of the odd moments for recollection and prayer.

8. The habit of recollection helps a person to concentrate during a prayer-time, and to realize in experience the truth of God's perpetual presence.

Notes

[1] The non-biblical quotations in this chapter are from *The Practice of the Presence of God*—Brother Lawrence.

PRAYING AND WORKING

14

The active and the contemplative life

On one occasion the Lord Jesus Christ was entertained in the home of Lazarus, and his two sisters Martha and Mary, in the village of Bethany just outside Jerusalem. Martha, busily engaged in the preparation of an elaborate meal, was irritated by the behavior of her younger sister, who sat at the feet of Jesus and kept listening to His word. She protested, "Lord, do you not care that my sister has left me to serve alone? Tell her then to help me." Jesus replied, "Martha, Martha, you are anxious and troubled about many things; one thing is needful. Mary has chosen the good portion which shall not be taken away from her" (Luke 10:38 to 42). The Lord commends Mary for listening to the word of God; but we must be careful not to misunderstand His reply to Martha. It is certainly a gentle rebuke of fussiness. He probably meant of course that a simple meal would have been enough. But it is not a disparagement of service—it follows the parable of the Good Samaritan!

Among the disciples of Christ are people of very different temperament. The contrast may not be so pronounced as in the case of Martha and Mary, but the differences undoubtedly exist. Some people are naturally quiet and contemplative. They like to sit, read, think, meditate, pray. For them, the discipline of prayer is comparatively easy. Others, no less devoted to the Lord, would rather be up and doing. These are the practical people, expressing devotion in action, loyalty in service.

What about you? To which group do you belong? Where do your sympathies lie—with Martha or with Mary? Most people in the Western world have a sneaking sympathy for Martha! But the best comment on this story has been made by St. Teresa. "To render our Lord a perfect hospitality, Martha and Mary must combine." They must be combined in each one of us. The life of prayer must find expression in service, contemplation must be translated into action, worship into work.

Worship and service in the Bible

Martha and Mary are certainly combined throughout the Scriptures, where no distinction is to be found between the worship and the service of God. Both in the Hebrew of the Old and the Greek of the New Testament, the same word is translated into English sometimes as "worship," sometimes as "service." Here are two examples of the way in which the Authorised Version and the Revised

Standard Version variously translate the same original. Describing his vision to the crew and passengers of the storm-tossed ship, Paul says, "for this very night there stood by me an angel of the God to whom I belong, and whom I *worship*" (R.S.V.) . . . "God, whose I am and whom I *serve*" (A.V.). The same apostle writes to the Romans, "present your bodies as a living sacrifice, holy and acceptable to God, which is your spiritual *worship*" (R.S.V.) . . . "which is your reasonable *service*" (A.V.). These are both good translations, and both are needed to do full justice to the original meaning (Acts 27:23; Romans 12:1).

To worship God is to serve Him; to serve Him is to worship Him. In the Old Testament, the chief act of worship was the offering of sacrifice. But in the New Testament the metaphor of sacrifice is not confined to what we today call "acts of devotion." Not only is it used of the spiritual sacrifices of praise and prayer (I Peter 2:5), but also of sharing our resources with needy people (Hebrews 13:16), of money gifts (Philippians 4:18), of evangelistic activity (Romans 15:16), and of the dedication of the whole personality to God's service (Romans 12:1). No distinction is drawn between acts of devotion expressed in praise and prayer, and acts of devotion expressed in service and work. Martha and Mary are combined. The worshipper is the servant of the Lord.

From the mountain-top to the valley

If the prayer life is to be fruitful, we must exhibit

this unity of prayer and service, worship and work, which is found in the Bible. Something is radically wrong if a healthy person spends a lot of time in prayer, and yet never seeks to express that devotion in practical service to God and man. This was not the example of Christ. He went up the mountain to pray. The enraptured Peter, desiring to prolong the communion with God, wanted to make three dwellings, so that Jesus, Moses and Elijah might *stay* there. The offer was not accepted. A distracted father and his epileptic son were waiting at the foot of the mountain, and Christ went down from intimate and exalted prayer to effective service.

But while there are some who pray without serving, there are many more nowadays who serve without praying. The modern world is full of folk who are "distracted with much serving, anxious and troubled about many things." Never was there so much ineffective service. Much of it is well-intentioned yet futile, because it is impotent to deal with the evil in man. The nine apostles who did not pray on the mountain-top, could not cast the demon out of the epileptic boy. They had to be told, "this kind cannot be driven out by anything but prayer" (Mark 9:29). Prayer is the secret of *effective* service. This unity, then, must be maintained both ways. Prayer must result in service and service find its inspiration in prayer. True worship must bear fruit in good work, and work itself be transformed into worship.

Serving the Lord

In many churches, it is usual for the minister to begin his sermon with the words, "in the name of the Father and of the Son and of the Holy Spirit"; it is by His authority and for His glory that I now do this. But ought not a Christian to be able to say the same before beginning any job? "Whatever your task, work heartily, *as serving the Lord* and not men" (Colossians 3:23). Not only preaching a sermon, but addressing a political meeting; not only breaking bread at the Lord's Supper, but breaking stones to make a road; not only kneeling to pray, but kneeling to scrub the kitchen floor, can be done to the glory of God. The cleaning woman had grasped this truth when she said, "I put the Lord Jesus Christ into the shine on the door-knobs."

Beware of the widespread assumption that some activities are "religious" and "spiritual," while others are ordinary and common. A religious activity may be secular, as when a man preaches a sermon to enhance his own reputation. A common activity may be spiritual, as when Christ washed the feet of His apostles, the menial task of a domestic slave. Brother Lawrence taught us "that our sanctification did not depend upon *changing* our works, but in doing that for God's sake, which we commonly do for our own." And so, whether you are trimming the hedge, or writing a letter, shining your shoes, or working in a factory, lubricating your car, or saying your prayers—do all as well as you can, with the intention of pleasing God.

Worship and work

Right intention, doing everything as unto the Lord, breaks down the barrier between work and worship; they become like the two sides of a penny, two aspects of one whole.

In the very first recorded act of worship, Cain and Abel offered up to the Lord, the first-fruits of the field and the flock (Genesis 4:3-5). At the temple a pastoral and agricultural community offered to God the products of work—bread, wine, oil, corn, fruit, sheep, oxen. Worship was offering, and the offering was the fruit of labor. This relationship was preserved in the primitive Eucharist, at which all the people made gifts of bread and wine. Not only in the sanctuary, but in field and factory, in shop and office, in classroom and council chamber, our work is to be offered to God. The offering in church *represents* the dedication of all work and service to God. Divine service does not end with the Benediction!

To work is to pray. This does *not* mean that bustling activity and hard work are an acceptable substitute for meditation and prayer. After all, Martha was rebuked by Christ for that very mistake. Not all work is prayer, and work may never be a substitute for prayer. But all work done with the intention to please God, is prayer, and is *one* important way in which a busy person can worship. It is possible to worship with the hand and the brain, as well as with the lips.

How to turn work into worship

How can we turn service into prayer, work into worship? This is what is involved.

First, do all your work with *the right intention.* It was said of Brother Lawrence "that the most excellent method he had found of going to God, was that of doing our common business without any view of pleasing men, and (as far as we are capable) purely for the love of God." Unless this intention is present in our work, our prayers will be lacking in vitality and reality. A man cannot work for himself all week, and then switch over to the worship of God on Sunday. "No one can serve two masters . . . you cannot serve God and mammon" (Matthew 6:24). This is one of the main reasons why people give up prayer and worship. In the end, you have to serve God everywhere—or nowhere.

Second, do all your work *as well as possible.* Obviously you cannot please God by doing your work badly. No man can do more than his best; no man should do less. It is not possible to work badly and pray well. Shoddy work spoils the devotional life; good work quickens it. Set out then to do everything as well as you possibly can.

If Jesus built a ship, she would travel trim.
If Jesus roofed a barn, no leaks would be left by Him.

If Jesus made a garden, it would look like Paradise.
If Jesus did my day's work, it would delight His
Father's eyes.

Third, practice the presence of God in your
work, and *do it in fellowship with Him.* You cannot always be thinking of God when you are working, but you can sometimes. Remember that God is
working all the time, and part of His work is being
done in and through you. You can enjoy God's
fellowship when working, just as much as in
church. Indeed, it was said of Brother Lawrence
"that he was *more* united to God in his outward
employments, than when he left them for devotion
in retirement." Enjoy your work if possible, talk to
God occasionally while you are doing it, and remember that you are a fellow-worker with Him.

Then, *offer your work to God.* Remember that
worship is offering and what you offer is your
work. Daily work may also be consecrated to God
during the Quiet Time, with a prayer for wisdom,
strength and skill to do it well. When the offering is
dedicated in public worship, offer yourself and the
work of the coming week to God.

In all these ways the Martha and the Mary in us
can combine, to offer the Lord a perfect hospitality.

Remember that:

1. Prayer and service must be combined in our devotion to the Lord.

2. No distinction is made in the Bible between the

worship and the service of God.

3. Prayer without service and service without prayer are alike contrary to the example of Christ.

4. Work becomes part of the devotional life when it is done with the intention to please God.

5. We should serve the Lord in all that we do.

6. Worship is work offered up to God.

7. Man can concentrate on the worship of God by doing his work for God.

8. Work becomes worship when it is done with the right intention; as well as possible; in fellowship with God; as an offering to God.

PRAYING
AND LIVING

15

The holy is the common

"The greatest contribution of the Hebrew to religion is that he did away with it."[1] For the ancient pagan, the sacred was a small area of life, carefully fenced off from the common and the ordinary. His idol god dwelt in the temple which was holy, and a man went there to worship him, or to consult him through his appointed representative. The temple and its enclosure was sacred; outside all was common.

But the living God of the Bible is the creator of the universe and the Lord of history. As the creator and Lord of all life, He cannot be fenced off, or confined within the bounds of a special area called "the religious." He is concerned with wages as well as with prayers, with justice as well as with worship, with people and politics as well as with churches. Devotion to Him must find expression not only in prayers, private or public, but in every part of life. "Prayers, therefore, are so far from being a sufficient devotion, that they are the smallest parts of it. . . . But then, as words are but small things in themselves, as times of prayer are but little, if compared with the rest of our lives; so that devotion which consists in times and forms of prayer is but a very small thing, if compared to that devotion which is to appear in every other part and circumstance of our lives."[2]

Balanced devotion

What does it mean to express devotion in every part of our lives? This maintenance of spiritual balance or equilibrium is of vital importance. One of the outstanding characteristics of the Lord Jesus was the wide range of His interests. He was not a person with a one-track mind, with one absorbing interest called "religion." He was not pietistic or churchy. As is evident from His parables, He was keenly interested in every aspect of life. We can avoid the danger of pietism (not piety, which is a gift of the Spirit), of being self-consciously good, of being too religious in the bad sense, by drawing together all of our daily experience, "sacred" and "secular" into one life lived in relationship with God. For the committed Christian it is artificial to divide life up into compartments labeled "religion," "daily work," "relationships," "recreation," "education." Baron von Hügel wrote to his niece: "I want you, just because you long for religion, to continue to cultivate, to cultivate more carefully and lovingly, also the interests, the activities, that are not directly religious. And this, not simply because 'why, of course, we must eat our dinner; of course, we must have our little relaxations'; but, much more, because, without these, you lose the material for Grace to work in and on."

Home, work, society

Worship, study and work may be the ideal for a monastic community. But how can we offer a balanced and complete devotion to the Lord? We must do it within and through the three orders of creation—the family, daily work, and our common life in society.

Life begins and grows within the family. Devotion which makes no difference to the way a person lives at home is obviously a fake. Relationship with the Lord should transform the relationships of the family, of husband and wife, parent and child, brother and sister. Prayer should enable a man to share fully in the joys and the responsibilities of the home. At a certain age, with school left behind, an adult enters the community of labor, the economic order. He takes some part in the processes of production, distribution and consumption, and helps to "maintain the fabric of the world." As he earns his living and supports a family, he contributes to the community. He must live as a responsible citizen of this world, rendering to Caesar the things that are Caesar's. He should be interested in his neighborhood, in social and civic issues, in politics and national life. Communion with God should result in "holy worldliness"—

responsible participation in the life of society. Withdrawal should be balanced by participation. The worship of God should result in the transformation of the three orders of creation—home, work and society.

Worship and the way we live

Prayer should influence the whole of life, and for the ordinary man today, that means life at home, at work and in society. This is only a way of saying that true prayer bears fruit in *good conduct.* Prayer and righteousness, devotion and lovingkindness, belong together. It was the assumption that they did not belong together, or could be divorced, that roused the indignation of the great Hebrew prophets. Many of their contemporaries assumed that what God required was simply a large number of "acts of devotion." If enough sacrifices were offered, according to the prescribed ritual, all would be well. God would be satisfied. But these devotional acts, though costly, had no influence on the way the worshippers lived. They had become substitutes for right personal relationships. But God is not pleased with a devotion which is separated from holy living. He *hates* such hypocrisy. "Your new moons and your appointed feasts my soul hates; they have become a burden to me, I am weary of bearing them . . . cease to do evil, learn to do good; seek justice, correct oppression; defend the fatherless, plead for the widow" (Isaiah 1:14, 16, 17). Not all prayer is acceptable to God, just because it is prayer. Devotional acts are hateful to God if they do not result in justice and practical love.

The teaching of the prophets is summed up in the great utterance "Behold, to obey is better than sacrifice, and to hearken than the fat of rams" (I Samuel 15:22). This does *not* mean that kindness and social justice are a substitute for worship—the heresy of the modern man. What God asks of us is obedience, of which worship and service, prayer and kindness, are all expressions. Note, not only the first and the second, but also the third part of Micah's well-known statement: "He has showed you, O man, what is good; and what does the Lord require of you but to do justice, and to love kindness, and to walk humbly with your God" (Micah 6:8).

We are to show our devotion to the Lord, not only in our prayers, but in our conduct—by the way we behave at home, at work and in the world. The love of a husband to his wife may be expressed in words of love or gratitude, of apology or request, corresponding to adoration, thanksgiving, confession and petition in prayer. But a wife would doubt the genuineness of words without thoughtfulness and kindness, helpfulness and generosity. Words may not be substituted for actions, nor actions for words.

So it is with loving the Lord—in prayer we speak, in living we act out our devotion. Helping with the chores at home, patiently teaching a new employee his job, designing a house, making dinner for the family of a neighbor who is ill, serving on the local city council, can all be acts of devotion to the Lord. And love grows by means of the acts which express it. *Doing our love* helps us in speaking our love.

Praying and loving

Because God is holy, those who live with Him must walk in newness of life. "You shall be holy, for I am holy (I Peter 1:15). But there is another reason why our love for Him must be expressed, not only in our prayers, but also in our personal relationships. We have to deal with God Himself in all our dealings with other people.

My relationship with God is not just vertical, it is also horizontal. I may find Him by going up the ladder of prayer. He is also in my neighbor, and I may meet Him there. *I have to deal with Him there.* In the parable of the Last Judgment, the good people show surprise when they are accepted and commended for having fed and clothed, entertained and visited Christ. Unwilling to enter the eternal kingdom under false pretences, they ask "Lord, when did we see thee?" The King replies, "As you did it to one of the least of these my brethren, you did it to me" (Matthew 25:31-46). They had been dealing with Christ Himself, in dealing with their needy brethren. Isn't this the most direct way in which we can love the Lord? "No man has ever seen God; *if we love one another, God abides in us and his love is perfected in us*" (I

John 4:12). These words were written to those who "believe in the name of his Son Jesus Christ," not to those who deliberately substitute good works for faith.

To those who believe and therefore pray, fellowship with God is lived out in love of our brothers. How difficult it is to pray when our relationships are wrong! Try for example, to pray after a quarrel, or when your conversation has been spiteful! On the other hand, when we encourage and give, help and serve, how easy it is to pray. Loving helps praying, just as praying helps loving.

Things that awaken love

By right living and by love (they are the same thing) we show our love and loyalty to God in the world. This love is primarily love for people—primarily, but not exclusively. In all the things which stir and quicken us to love, we may experience the presence of God. There are many times when God takes the initiative, and without any effort on our part, discloses Himself to us. All that is needed of us is recognition and a response of love. As George Macdonald says, "whatever wakes my heart and mind, thy presence is, my Lord." The mind may be quickened by some aspect of nature, of art, or daily life. A sunset or a symphony, a poem or a song, a deed of heroism or a scientific discovery may quicken the mind to an awareness of God. Listening to a lecture, reading a book, the devotion of a dog, an unexpected gift, a letter from a friend, any experience, fact or event, may be used by God, may be a stairway down which He comes to us.

Consecrating the commonplace

Prayer should transform the common life of the world, so that at last everything will be holy to the Lord. The Jewish people were accustomed to regarding certain places and times, certain objects and priests as especially holy. But the prophet Zechariah looked forward to the time when *everything* in the community would be sacred; when "religion" as a separate sphere, a department of life, would be abolished. "And on that day there shall be inscribed on the bells of the horses, 'holy to the Lord'." Not only the mitre of the high-priest upon which these words were inscribed but the common horses in the street—the cars, bicycles and buses of the ancient world—would be sacred to God. Not only the vessels of the altar "but every pot in Judah and Jerusalem shall be sacred to the Lord of hosts" (Zechariah 14:20, 21). This should be the goal for each of us. We must have our special times and places, our private prayers and church services; but the purpose of these is the consecration of the commonplace.

When John of Patmos looked through an open door into heaven, he saw no temple in the new Jerusalem. The entire city was the holy of holies! The presence of God had consecrated the whole. The aim of the devotional life has been realized when we can wholeheartedly sing with the seraphim: *Holy, holy, holy, Lord God of hosts, heaven and earth are full of thy glory. Glory be to thee O Lord most high. Amen.*

Remember that:

1. The whole of life must be devoted to the Lord.
2. A true Christian is not just interested in religion, but in the whole of life.
3. We should express our devotion to the Lord in the home, in our daily work, and in society.
4. Our holy God requires of His worshippers a holy life.
5. Devotion must be *done* as well as *said*.
6. One way we can love the Lord is by loving our fellow-men.
7. We can worship God through all the things that stir us to love.
8. The goal of devotion is to make all life holy.

Notes

[1] *Only One Way Left*—George F. Macleod (Iona Community).

[2] *A Serious Call*—William Law.